Sculpting Miniature Military Figures

with

Kim Jones

Schiffer Publishing Ltd

77 Lower Valley Road, Atglen, PA 19310

Text written with
and photography by
Douglas Congdon-Martin

ACKNOWLEDGEMENTS

None of us exists in a vacuum. We are all influenced by people that we feel the need to recognize as contributing to our success. The following is a list of those people. The order in which they appear has no bearing on their influence in my life.

I would like to express my heartfelt thanks to:
Mike Davidson, for getting me started in this addictive hobby!
Jon Maguire, for introducing me to Peter Schiffer.
David Butterfield, for his art work and suggestions.
My family, for their support and faith in me.

DEDICATION

This book is dedicated to my parents, Jay and Frances Jones, for instilling in me a love of history and art, and to my fiancee, Loretta Chisum, for keeping me going when I just knew I couldn't take another step.

CONTENTS

Copyright © 1994 by Kim Jones
Library of Congress Catalog Number: 94-66367

Printed in China
ISBN: 0-88740-626-2

We are interested in hearing from authors with book ideas on related topics.

Published by Schiffer Publishing Ltd.
77 Lower Valley Road
Atglen, PA 19310
Please write for a free catalog. This book may be purchased from the publisher. Please include $2.95 postage.
Try your bookstore first.

INTRODUCTION

The art of creating military miniatures is centuries old. The pharaohs of a ancient Egypt commanded miniature warriors to be carved and included in their tombs to guard them on their journey across the great river. Frederick the Great had lead soldiers made for his children's play. More recently, a man by the name of W.R. Britain began production of toy soldiers in the late 1800s. Britain developed a method of hollow casting and mass producing toy soldiers which made them affordable. Entire regiments could be assembled and displayed in the space of a table top. While commercial castings of soldiers have been available from manufacturers since Britain's time, it is within the last twenty years that the hobby of sculpting military miniatures has experienced an upsurge in popularity.

Commercial castings of military miniatures are, by necessity, somewhat stoic in their appearance. The casting process forces certain limitations on the animation of the human figure. While recent innovations in casting techniques and new, lighter casting materials have breathed new life into commercial figures, there is still that desire on the part of the consumer to want that figure in a little different position or to have the figure wearing a different type of tunic. From this desire to create something unique, to add that personal touch to a military miniature, many people have resorted to converting commercial castings by reanimating the pose or redressing the figure. Once the apprehension of ruining a fifty dollar figure is overcome, the possibilities are limitless!

When extensive conversion has been done on a casting, it begins to become clear that the only reason for purchasing a ready-made figure is so that the artist has an armature from which to begin. It is a logical step from this beginning to sculpting your own military miniatures. Rather than using an expensive casting as an armature, you can simply use brass rod upon which to build your own figure. Tools, techniques and materials for sculpting military miniatures are nearly as varied as the types of soldiers that you can create. Each artist has his own methods when it comes creating a figure. In this book I will show you how I have sculpted military miniatures for the past ten years. I will suggest various ways to achieve the same end and I am sure that the reader will develop his or her own techniques and materials to create one-of-a-kind military miniatures.

THE PROJECT

Normally I like to sculpt figures that show the military man in his relaxed state, doing things that would make up his everyday life. However, on this project I decided to portray a U.S. cavalryman during a winter campaign against the Cheyenne. I wanted to create a miniature with action and drama so I decided to position him in the snow, sliding down a ravine, trying to evade his imagined enemy. To help add drama to the scene I wanted to show his coat tails and cape blowing in the wind. The accompanying sketch gives a rough idea of the intended position and look of the finished figure. Now on to the sculpting!

FRONT

SIDE

SLOPE

BEFORE SCULPTING

Before you start modeling figures, it is important to get to know your medium. Whether it is Sculpy, Fimo, or epoxy putty, which is my preference, it is important to be familiar with how it molds, dries, cures, and its possibilities and limitations. This is a two-part epoxy putty, blended together in equal amounts by kneading.

The armature is made from 1/8" brass welding wire. This is available at reasonable prices from welding supply houses. When I began, I used hanger wire. The welding wire comes in 3 foot sections, but I cut it to 1 foot lengths for convenience.

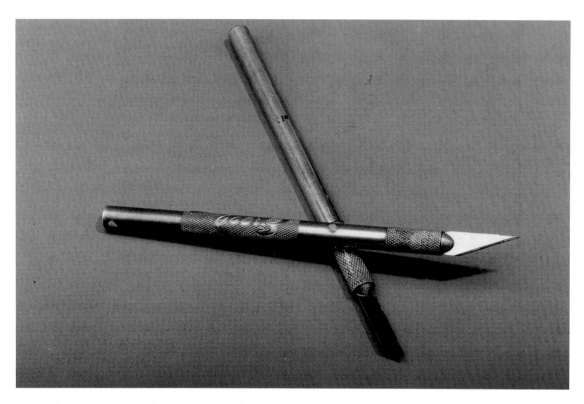

Tools will range from Exacto knives and saws...

to small files and jeweler's chisels or gravures...

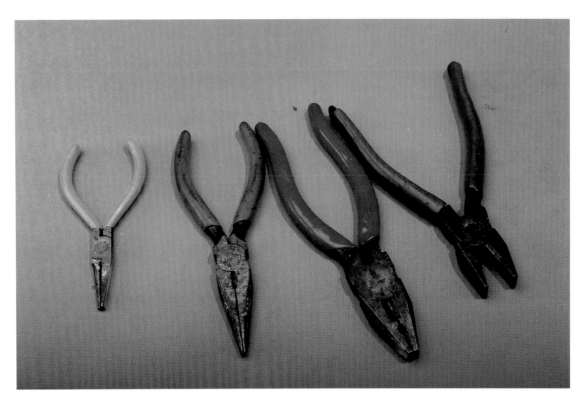

and various sized pliers. The heavier pliers are for cutting and bending the armature wire. The needle nosed pliers are also good for making tighter bends. The ring pliers on the left (yellow handle) have a round jaw and a flat jaw. The round jaw allows you to make rings from the wire.

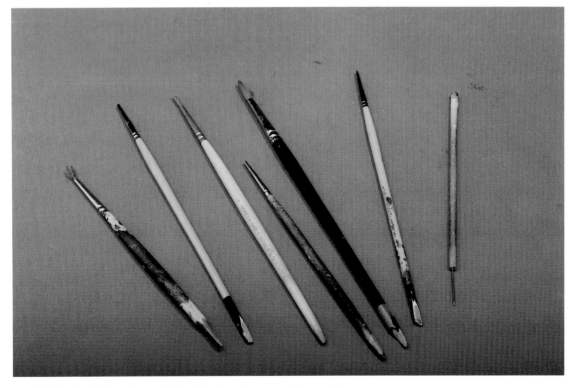

All the tools I use for sculpting the clay I have made myself from the handles of old paint brushes. Commercially made tools are available, but they are generally too large for the miniature work. I just carve and sand the shapes, then coat them with epoxy glue to give a smooth, non-porous surface

The main tool I use is shaped like a butter knife.

Another comes to a point like a pencil.

A hook shaped tool is used for making folds, wrinkles and other details.

Other handles are made into assorted chisel shapes. These make finer wrinkles and cuffs around the wrists, and are used for defining lines and other details.

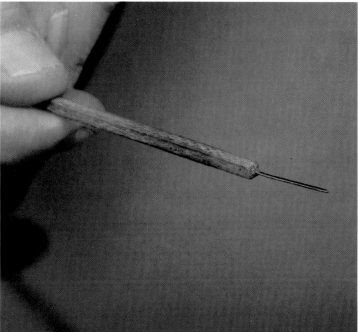

A pin epoxied into the end of a stick is used for making eyes, texturing hair, and finer work.

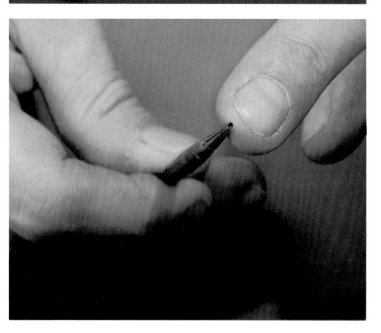

Removing the hair from the end of a brush will give you a nice tool for forming buttons. You will need to drill the hairs out of the hole.

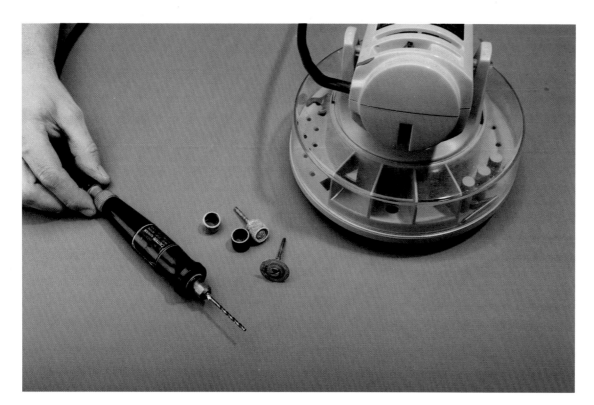

A rotary tool with various bits is used mainly for sanding, cutting and drilling.

This simple oven is used to cure the epoxy putty quickly, about 15 minutes. This thing gets hot, so don't use more than a 60 watt bulb or you will burn the box.

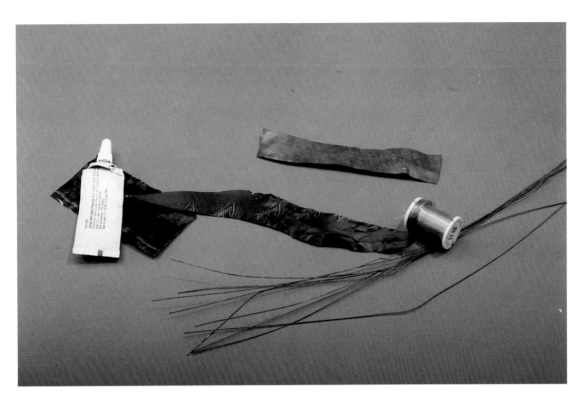

Other materials include tin and lead sheets, and thin wire. The tin sheets can be recycled from old tubes of medicine, and the lead sheets are available at plumbing supply houses. The spool wire can be found at a hardware store and the other, florist's wire, can be found at most craft stores. You will see how they are used later in the book.

To get the best results at sculpting figures you need as much reference material as you can find, not only historical, but anatomical.

SCULPTING THE FIGURE

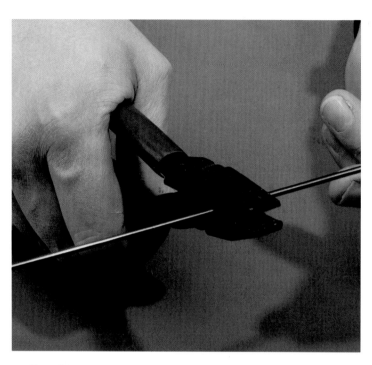

I work in 125mm scale or about 1/16 scale. I start with a wire approximately 8" long. It's better to be too long than too short.

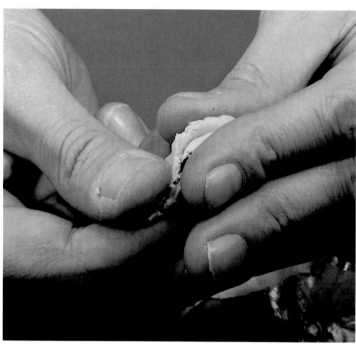

Knead them together...

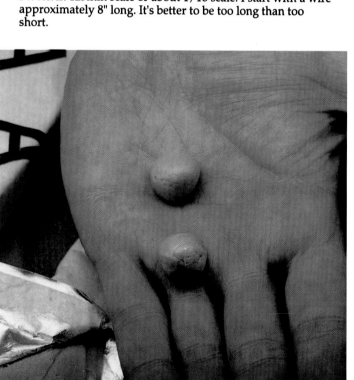

Mix up as much putty as you can comfortably use in 30 minutes. Start with equal balls of parts A & B.

until the color is uniform. It is better to knead it more than less.

Keep your hands clean or the excess putty will get in the way.

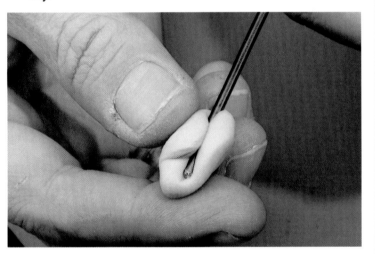

Begin the head by wrapping a ball of putty around the end of the 8" armature. I start with the head because it establishes the scale for the rest of the sculpture.

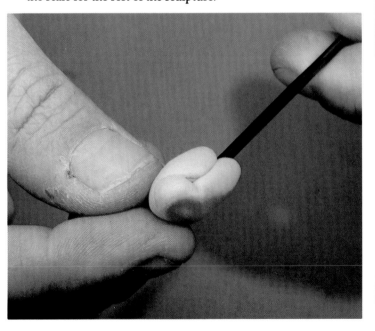

Work it until well-rounded and smooth.

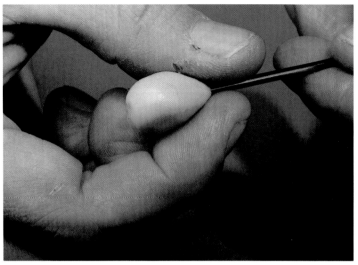

Form it into a tear drop shape.

Place it in the oven for about 15 minutes. A word of caution. In the oven the putty can actually get softer and sag just before it hardens. Keep an eye on it to be certain it doesn't sag into a shape you cannot use. Also, when you remove a piece from the oven let it cool thoroughly or run it under cold water before applying any new putty. The heat will make any added putty unmanageable.

The hardened tear drop acts as a base for the rest of the head sculpture. Apply a snake of putty to this...

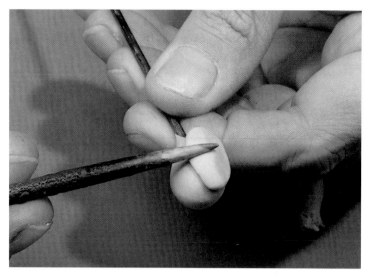

and roll it out with a tool or with your finger.

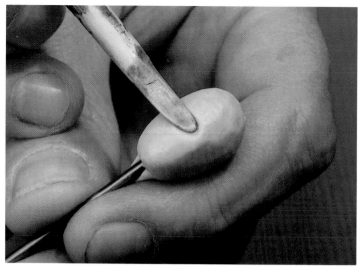

Switch to a paddle tool to make the details of the face. Start with eye sockets. If you are right handed, start with the figure's right eye and push in.

This will make a mask from which the face will be sculpted. There is a hint of a chin.

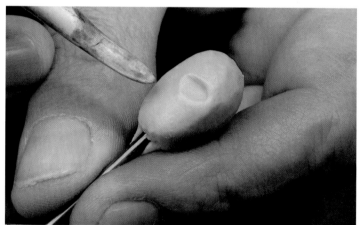

The result.

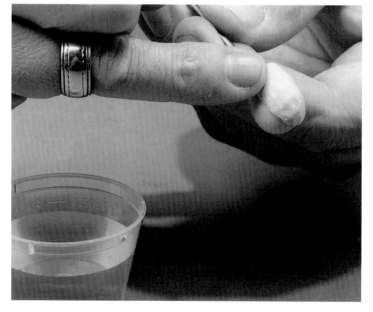

A moistened finger will smooth the surface. It is good to have water handy to keep your tools moist. This will greatly ease the working of the putty.

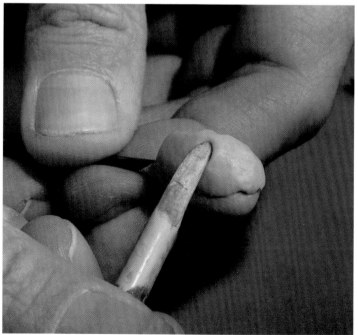

Repeat on the other side.

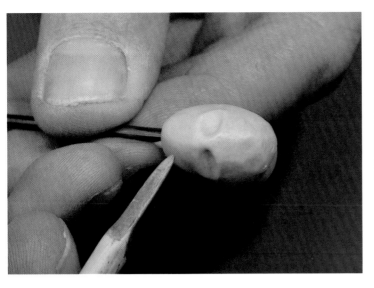

The result.

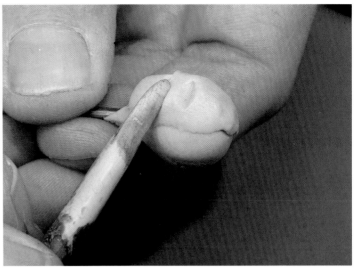

In the same way, form the cheek bones, pushing up only slightly. Do both sides.

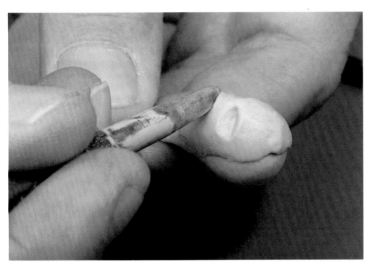

Give a hint of the nose by pushing in with the edge of the paddle at the upper lip and pushing up to the underside of the nose.

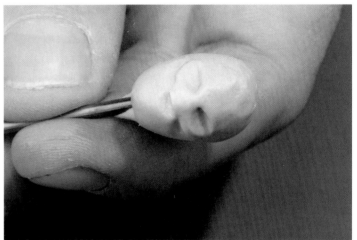

The result.

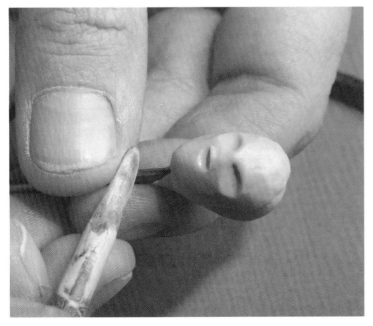

The result.

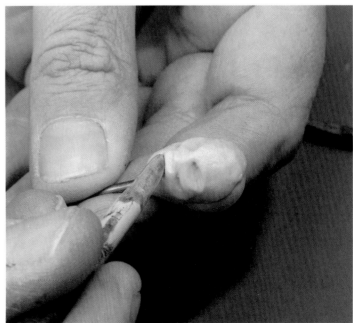

This figure has an open mouth, so I push in below the upper lip and pull down.

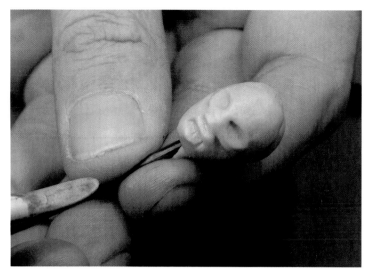

Result.

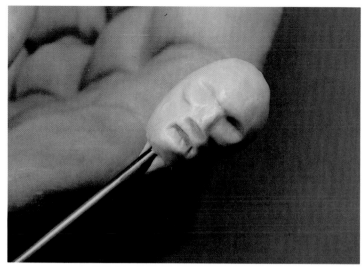

Ready to be baked. If you do too much before hardening, you are going to create some misshaping.

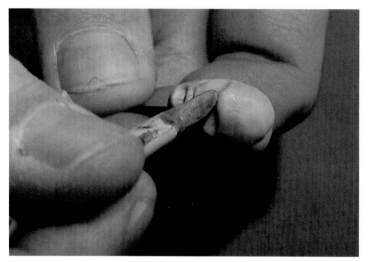

Push up at the bridge of the nose to create a brow.

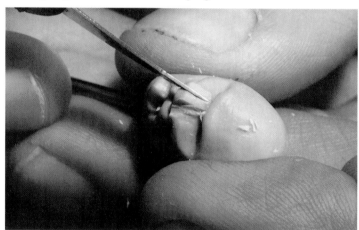

When the head has hardened, use the Exacto knife to shape the features. I begin by thinning the nose on each size, cutting into the cheek.

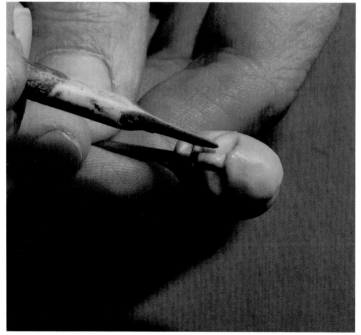

Bring the nose up by pushing in from the sides.

Trim down the cheeks to get a nice transition from the nose.

Hollow out the face under the cheek bone.

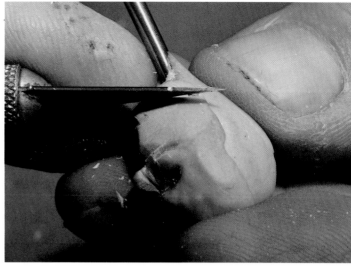

Cut straight into the jaw line...

Progress. The jaw will have to be thinned on one side for the face to be symmetrical.

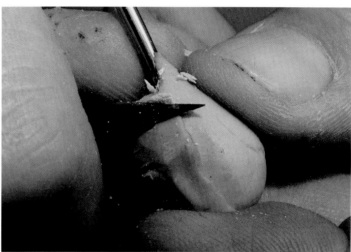

and trim from the line back to the neck to define the jaw. Repeat on the other side.

Curl under the bottom lip to bring out the chin.

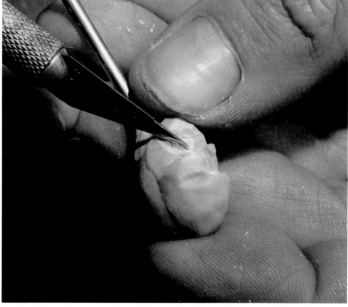

Establish a smile line from the nostril down beside the mouth.

Shape the forehead back to the brow.

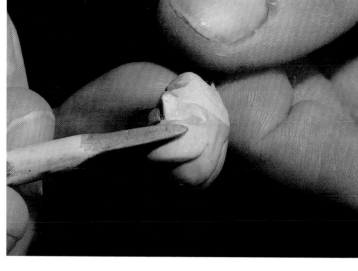

Blend it in with the brow using a paddle tool.

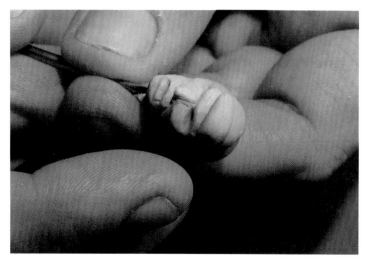

With the basic shapes set, lay another small snake of epoxy putty on the brow. This can be more than you need.

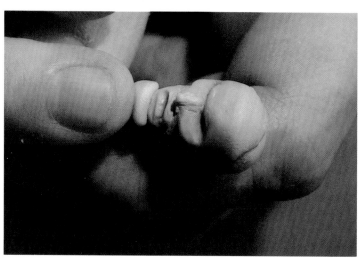

In the same way add to the chin, using more putty than you will need.

Roll it out to add some body to the forehead.

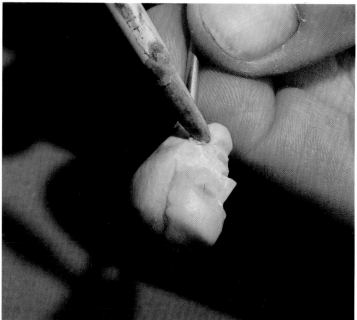

Blend it into the face.

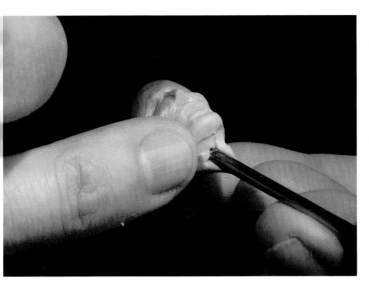

A moistened finger helps smooth and shape. You want to get it even, but if it isn't, you can come back and harden it up.

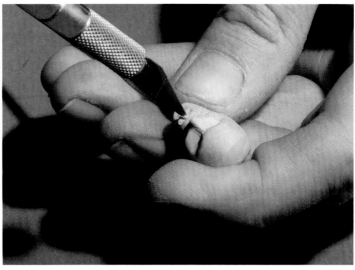

This figure has his mouth open, in panic or yelling to his comrades. To create this effect I use the Exacto knife as a drill. This makes a hole without damaging the upper lip. The lower lip is not of concern because we will be working with it later.

Progress front...

This takes you to this point.

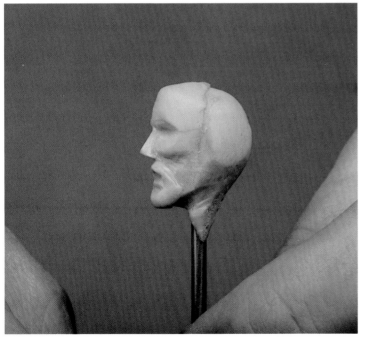

and side.

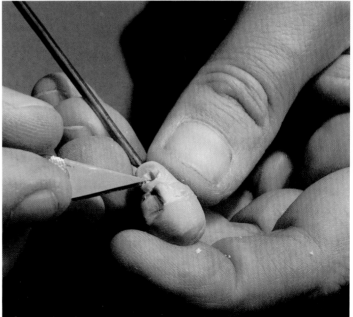

Carve out the corners, working toward the upper lip, but not into it. Shape the upper lip to be sure it is even.

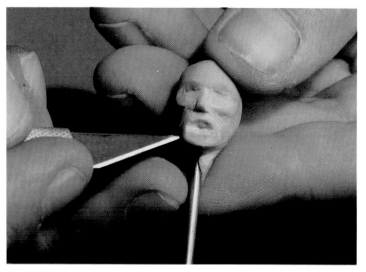

Progress.

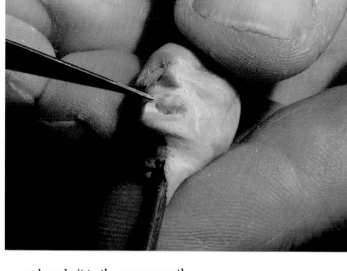

and apply it to the upper mouth.

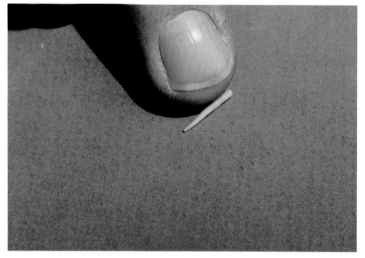

Some teeth add to the dramatic effect. Roll a snake of putty.

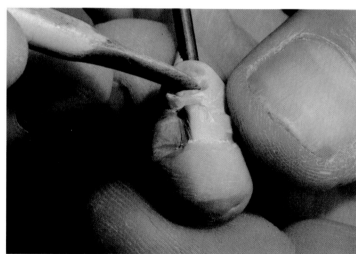

Shape it into teeth.

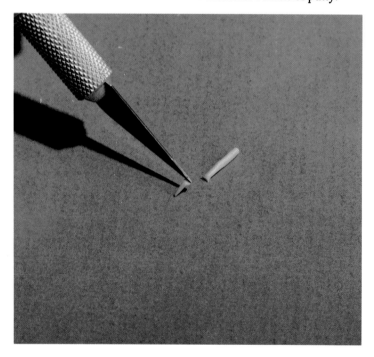

Cut off a small part of the snake...

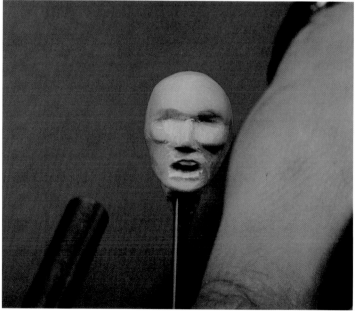

The result is just a hint of teeth. You don't need to worry about individual teeth unless you want to show one missing. In that case you would let things dry, then carve it out.

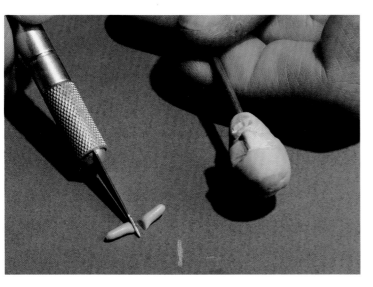

I'm going to fill in the cheeks and better define the jaw line. A good way to be sure the face stays balanced is to make a snake and divide it in half, one half for each side of the face.

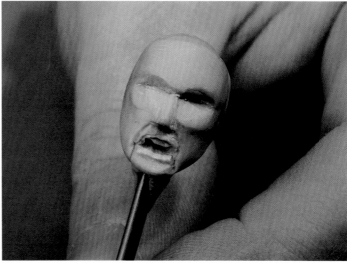

You want to keep the frown line, and may even want to accentuate it as it comes down from beside the nostril. This adds character to this part of the face.

I just lay it under the cheek bone and fair it in. This leaves a frown line. Repeat on the other side.

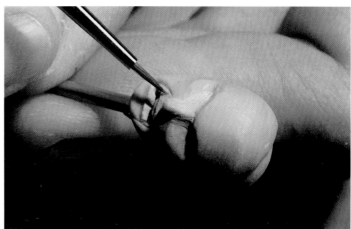

The hard tools sometimes leave hard lines. You can sculpt with a moist brush to soften the lines.

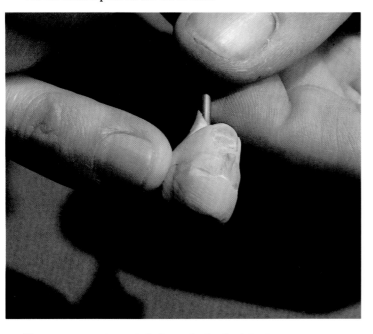

Since we are not worried about the back of the head at this point, it is a good place to drag the excess putty.

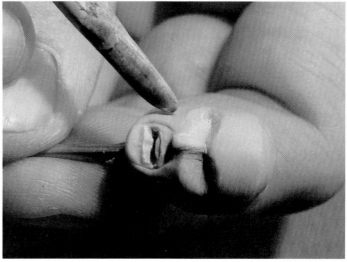

While the cheeks are soft you can use the paddle tool to add some dimples, giving even more character to the face. Again, soften these lines with a brush. These lines and details in the face add character and drama to the piece, and can be used to add age.

The bottom lip is created in a similar way to the teeth. Roll a thin snake and cut off a piece.

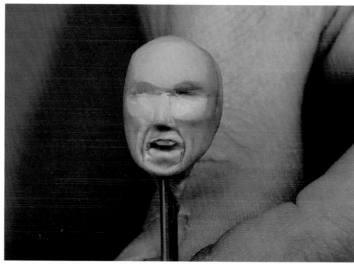

Ready for the oven.

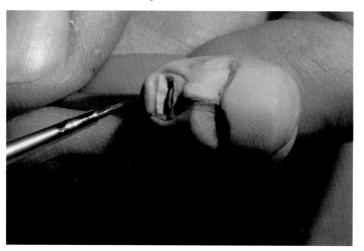

Put it in place...

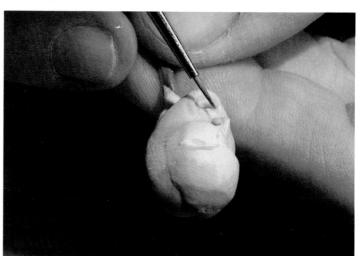

Blend a small bit of putty to form the nostril.

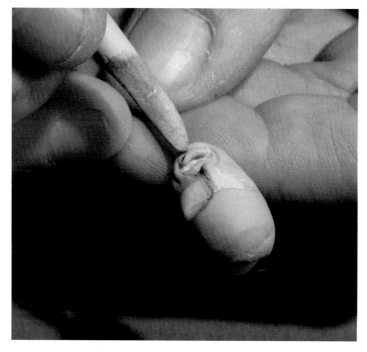

and shape it.

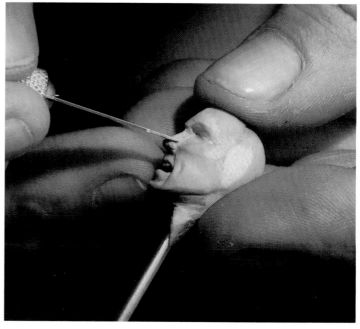

It's better to use a little more putty than you need, because you can trim it away.

From a snake of putty cut two equal size pieces for the eyeballs.

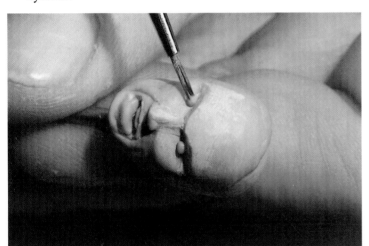

Situate them in the eye sockets so they are equally spaced, approximately centered on the corners of the mouth.

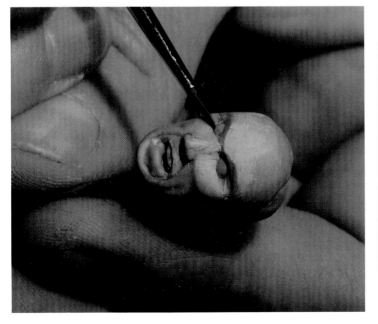

Spread and shape the eyeballs with the brush. You can fix any inequality in the sizes of the eyeballs at this point.

Progress. You might be tempted to use a pinhole for the pupil of the eye, as would be done in larger sculpture. I would not recommend it, because it makes painting more difficult.

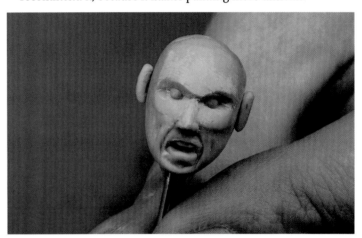

Although the ears are covered in the model we are building, you should know how to sculpt them. Begin with two equally sized pieces of putty. They are applied to the front edge of the ear aligned with the back of the jaw line, and the top aligned with the eyes.

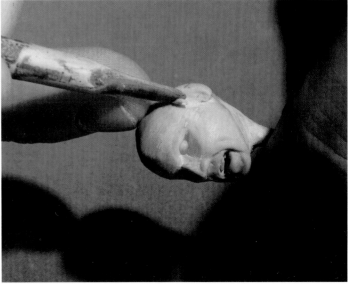

Establish an oval shape and fair in the front edge.

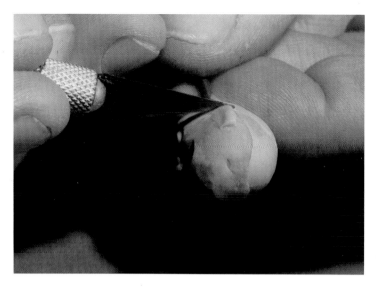

Size the ears, making sure they are symmetrical.

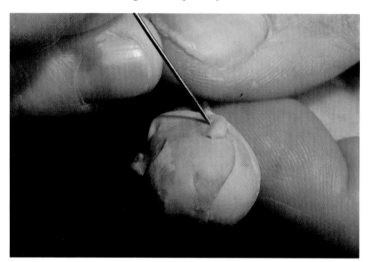

Establish an ear canal and the details of the ears contours. It's best to look at an ear as a reference.

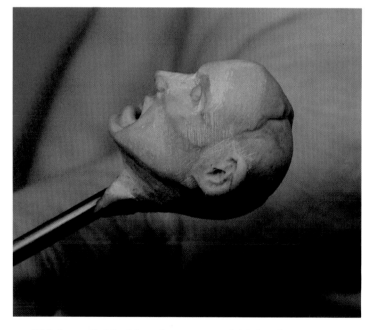

This is not finished, but shows some of the details you can use.

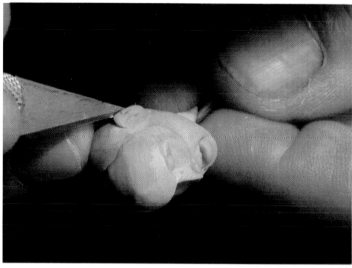

The previous steps have pushed the ear against the head. While it is in this position we trim edges and make refinements to it.

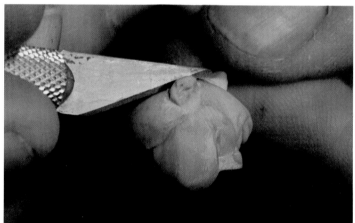

When you are satisfied with the ear, come behind it and push it out from the head so you don't get the pinned back look. If the details close up, you can open them with the point of your brush.

Ready for baking.

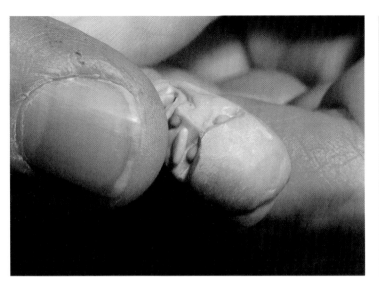

When it has hardened we will go back to the eyes. Roll out a snake and apply part of it to the lower lid. You can start out with more than you need and work it away.

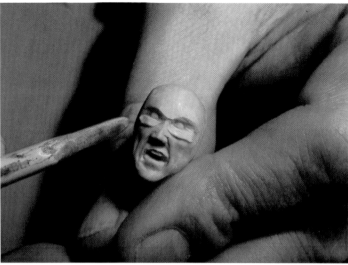

That takes care of the mass. Now we need to blend and shape the bags.

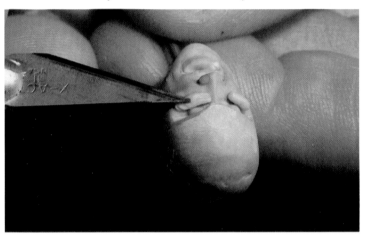

Press it into place.

One side trimmed and blended. The eyes can be adjusted depending on the age or the conditions under which they live.

As you work it, the important thing is to keep from covering up the eyeball. As a rule the bottom lid is relatively straight where it meets the eye.

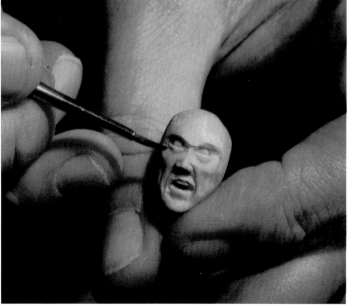

The lower lids of both eyes done.

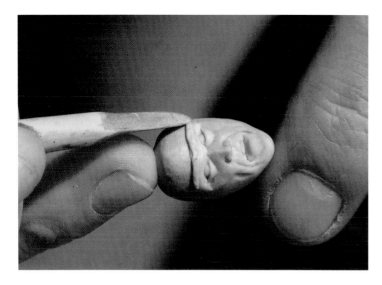

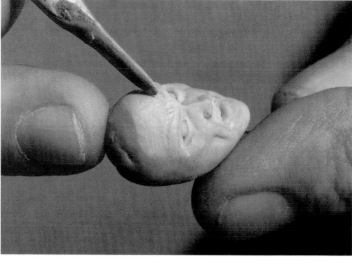

Work in a snake of putty to form a brow ridge. Similar to the lower lip, we are going to blend it in on the bottom side, toward the eye ball...

and some "Oh God, what kind of trouble am I in!" furrows in the brow.

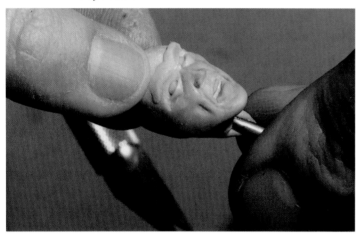

then pull it up into the forehead. This serves two purposes. It establishes the brow line and gives us some extra putty for wrinkles and lines.

The result. The furrows do not need to be carried too high because there will be a hat.

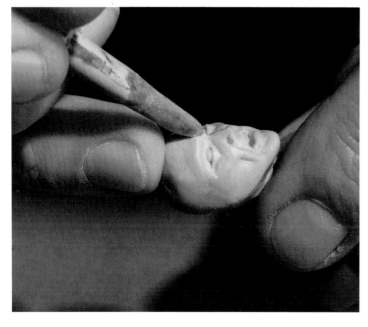

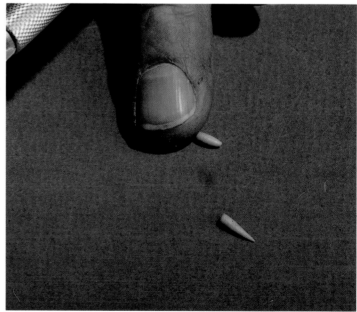

Create a separation in the middle of the brow...

The moustache is made from two snakes, rolled so the ends are pointed.

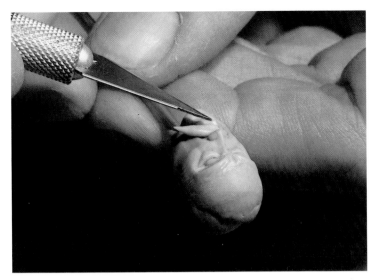

Cut it to the right size, lay it on, and work it into place.

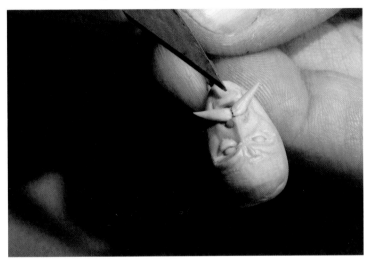

Repeat on the other side.

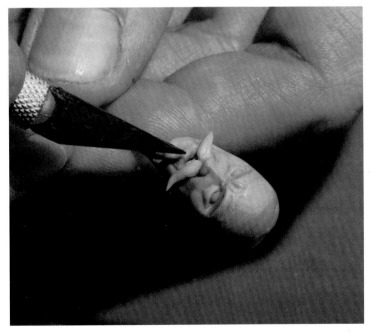

Shape and trim the moustache. Make sure you don't lose the teeth and that they still are visible.

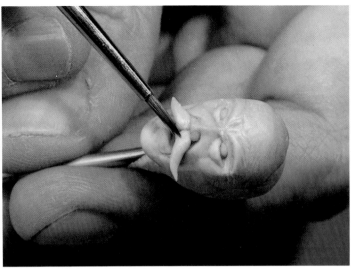

While there is a division between the sides of the moustache, you don't want it to be too deep or the face will take on a feline look. Use a brush to shape it.

Ready to bake. Remember the epoxy has a tendency to sag in the oven. Check it to be sure that things stay in alignment.

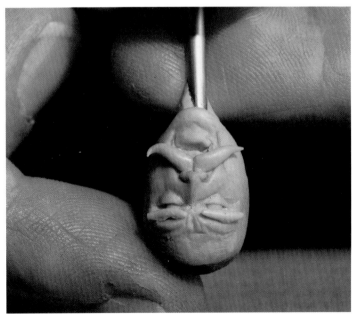

When the putty has set and cooled, lay on putty for the upper lid of the eye.

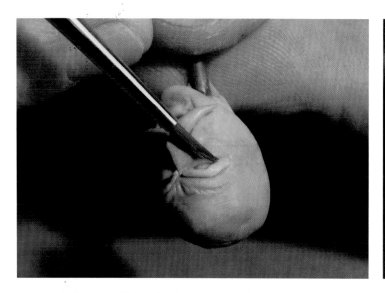

Arch the upper lid so that it goes around the eye and meets the lower lid in the corners.

Trim the lid down and sculpt it with a knife. Here you can see one side complete.

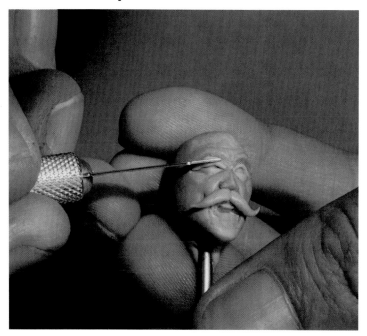

Repeat on the other side.

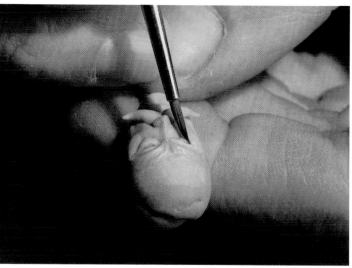

Shape it with a brush. You don't want to close the eye too much or you will have a difficult time painting. Besides this guy's eyes have a fearful, open look to them. At the same time he is aiming a pistol, which tends to make one squint.

Both eyes done. Note how the upper lid comes over the lower at the corners.

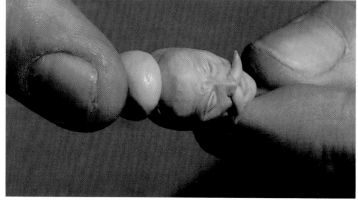

The hat starts as a large ball of putty at the crown.

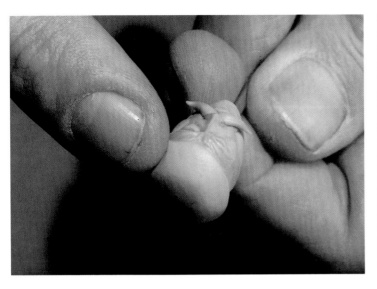

With a slightly moistened finger work it over the head with a turning, tapping, rolling motion.

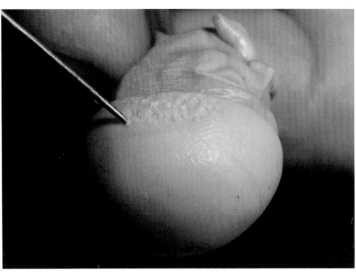

The hat was originally made of muskrat, so I create a texture by picking at it lightly with a needle, using a stick-and-lift motion.

As you work on a piece of historical clothing, like this hat, it is important to make regular reference to your sources. This source is *The Horse Soldier* by Randy Steffen.

Go back and push down some of the peaks to soften the texture.

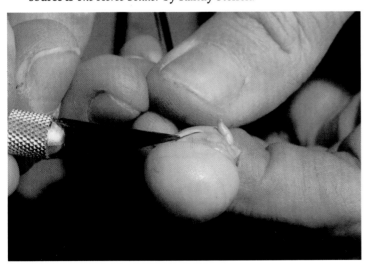

Use a knife to establish the contours of the bottom of the hat.

Back in the oven.

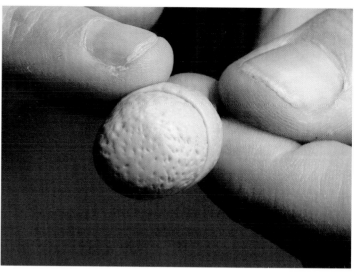

Sometimes you want to let the putty set for awhile before you use it. The flaps of the hat, which you want to hang away from the head is one such place. The putty is at the state of warm wax. Roll it into a snake and wrap it around the back of the head at the bottom of the hat.

and your finger to smooth it out.

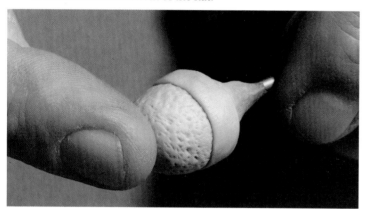

Flatten it out.

Trim it up where it meets the crown of the hat.

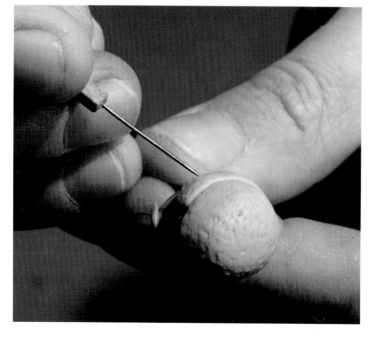

Texture it as you did the top of the hat, using a pin to prick it...

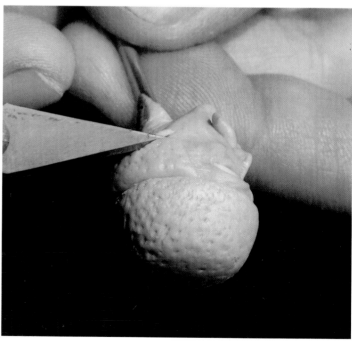

Shape it to the correct style for the cap.

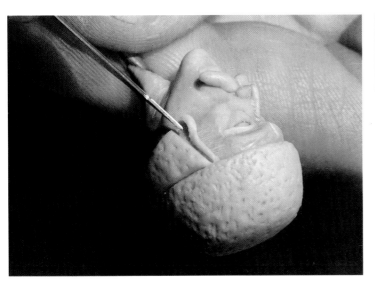

Undercut the front edge of the flap to make it appear thinner.

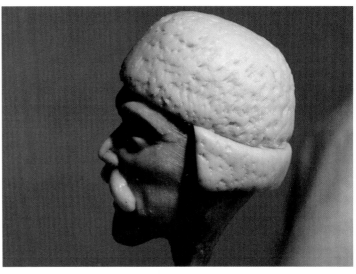

The flaps need a little more shaping.

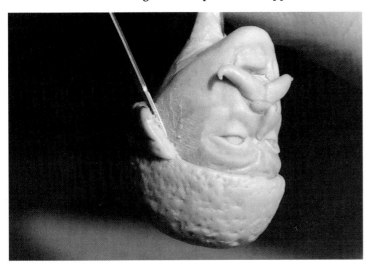

Run the blade under the flap and lift it away from the head in a curl.

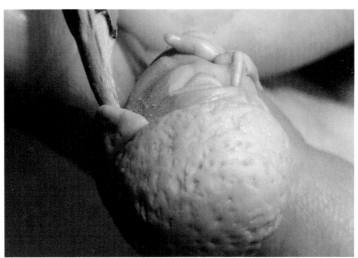

Lift the flap so they look like they are flapping in the breeze. Remember we will be adding full sideburns underneath. The putty at this state is quite pliable, and can be shaped a lot without fear of breaking. If you had enough, you could make a furled flag.

Progress.

The finished flaps. I spend time on the flaps because they help create the illusion of the wind blowing, and give the piece the kind of tension and drama I'm after.

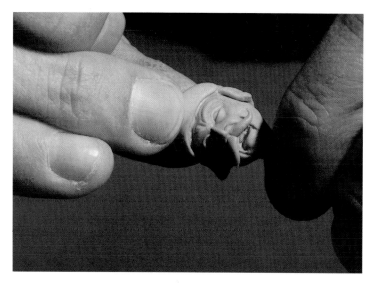

The front flap is created in the same way.

Texture the trim and slip your knife behind it to pull it away from the crown, giving the hat a three dimensional look.

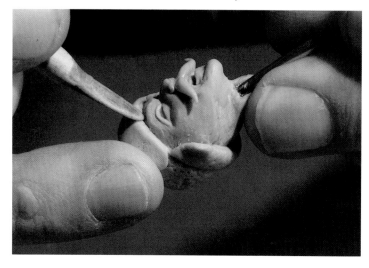

Push it up to the forehead to make sure it looks like it is attached.

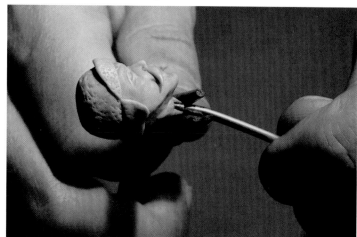

If you are doing this for the first time it will be helpful to have a good anatomy book with drawings of the body in various positions. We are going to bend the armature wire to the position our figure will be taking. He is looking back over his right should with his left leg extended straight. Make a bend back under the head.

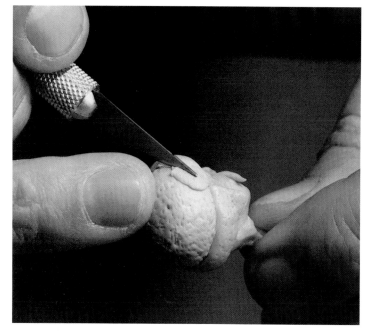

Cut it to the proper shape.

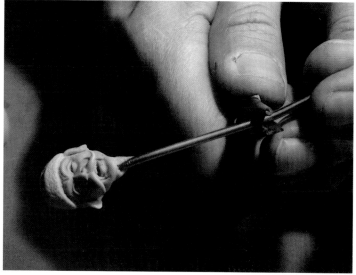

There is another slight bend in the hip...

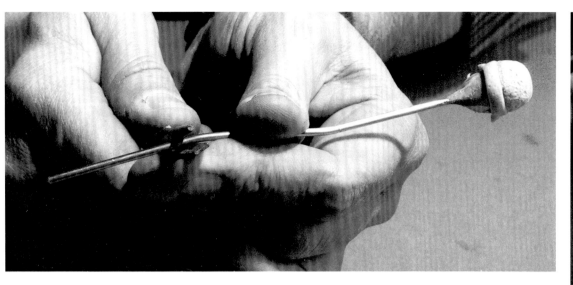

and a bend at the knee.

Add another lump for the hip joint. Since the wire is going to be in the left leg we want to keep the bulk of the torso and hip blocks to the left. Bake these basic blocks.

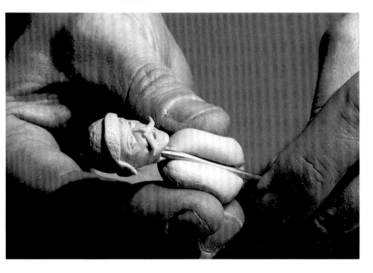

Wrap putty around the rod to create a base for the chest and shoulders.

Shape it in a roughly triangular shape.

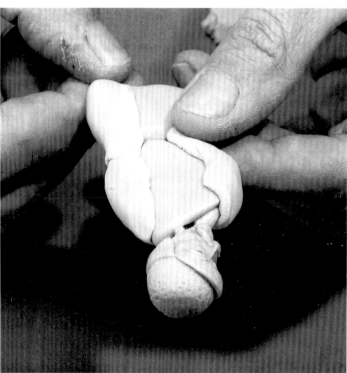

I like to fill out the side shapes of the body before working on the thickness. The object is to build-up the body so the final layer is just clothing. If you put to much depth at this point, when you come to the clothing it is more likely that the figure will look unnaturally stuffed.

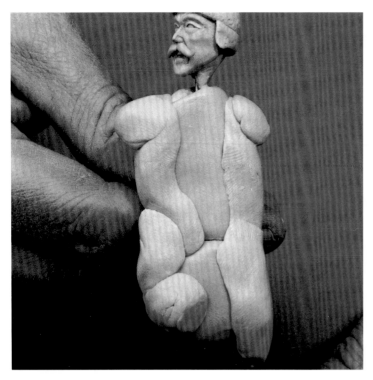

You want to have masses at the shoulder and calves into which you will drill to add wires for the limbs. Bake this portion before proceeding.

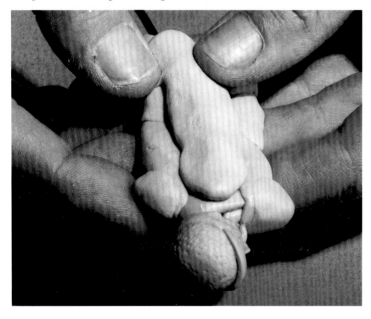

Now we beef the figure out front to back. While you are doing this it is good to have the anatomy references out to help you keep an eye on proportions and body structure. Begin by adding a snake of putty to the front and spreading it out. Don't worry if it gets a little disproportionate, because we are going to come back and shape it.

Two views showing how much beef we add at this point. Bake it before continuing.

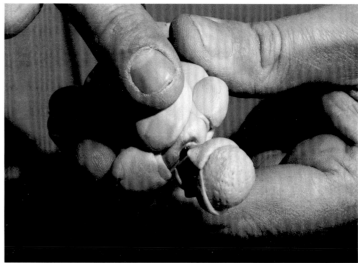

Do the same thing to the back.

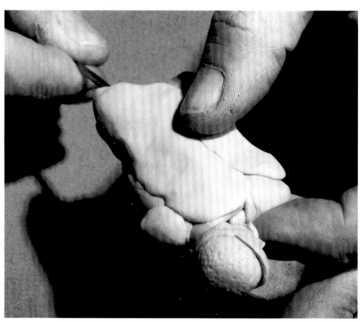

Continue to add where it needs it, like here under the arm.

 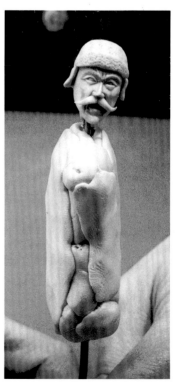

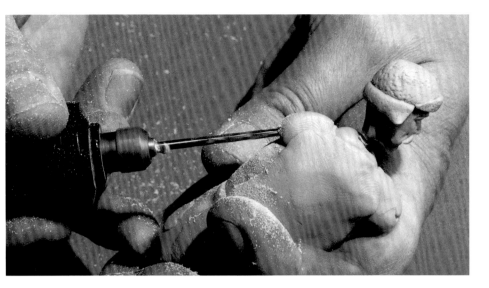

Drill holes for the limb armatures. They should follow the angle that the arm or leg will have as it comes away from the body. The holes only need to be 1/8" to 1/4" deep.

The angles are in three dimensions. This right arm is pointed up and back as he aims over the shoulder.

The front right leg is in a propped up position, so the angle is up.

The rods for the limbs can start out a little long. They can be trimmed to size after the anatomy is established. For drastically bent limbs, liked the raised leg, it is good to have a really long wire so you have a handle to hold while you bend it. Hold it in place to establish where the bend will go. Here it will go where my thumb and forefinger are.

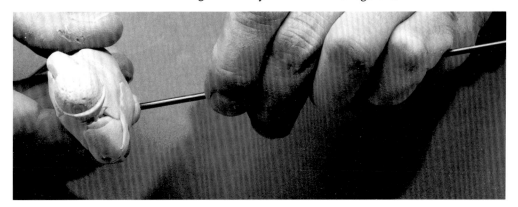

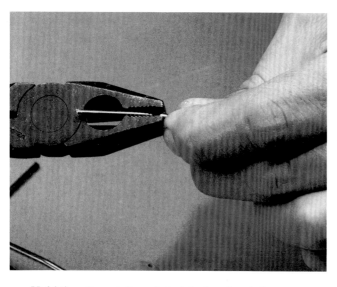

Hold the pliers at the point of the bend and shape the wire.

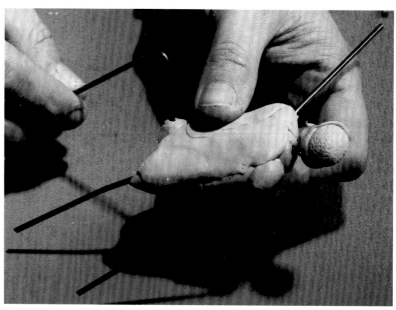

The armatures in place.

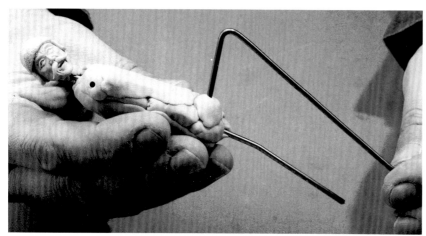

The left arm is fairly straight, but the hole we drilled was slightly off. To correct this kind of mistake you can make a bend right at the top of the armature. The other arm is straight.

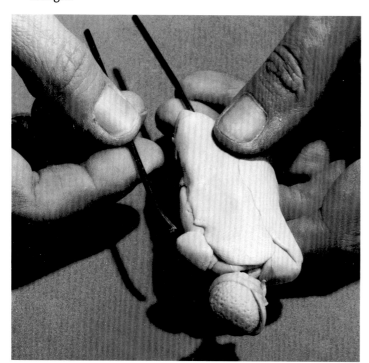

Before gluing trim them to length. Hold the arms in place and mark a spot that is approximately where the palm of the hands will be. This will leave a little extra to be trimmed later.

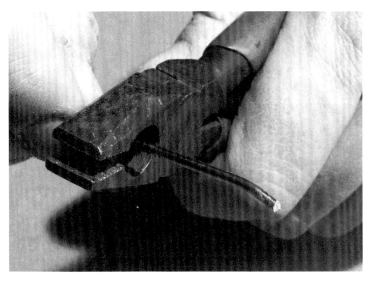

Clip it off.

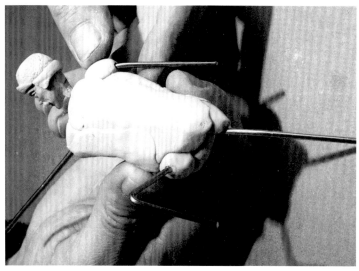

The armatures in place. The body is a little wide...

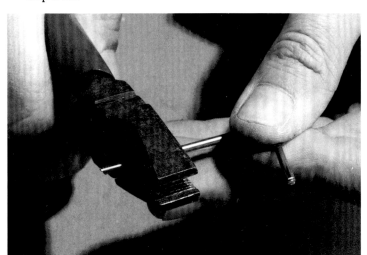

We leave the original leg at full length for now. If the figure were standing you would leave the leg wires longer than necessary so they could support the figure. Cut the bent leg at the length of the heel.

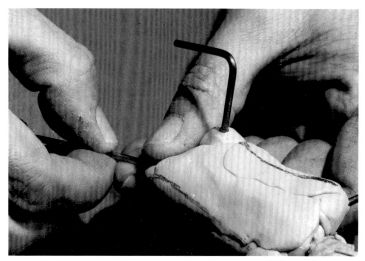

so we'll shape it with a rotary grinder, giving it the contour it needs. Mark the areas that need slimming.

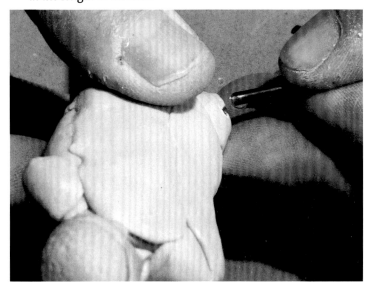

Super glue the limbs in place. It is better to put the glue on the rod than in the socket, because the glue could keep the wire from seating all the way in.

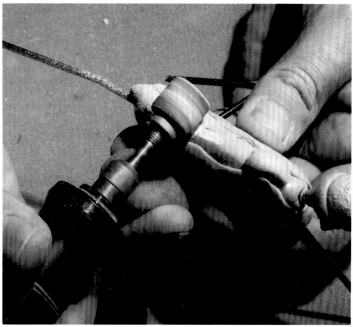

Grind the areas to be removed.

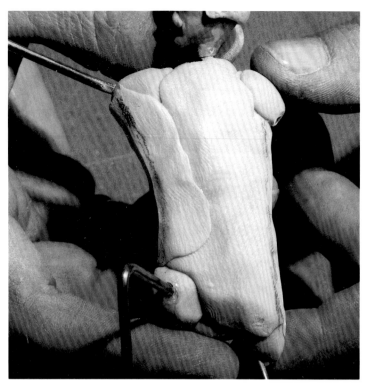

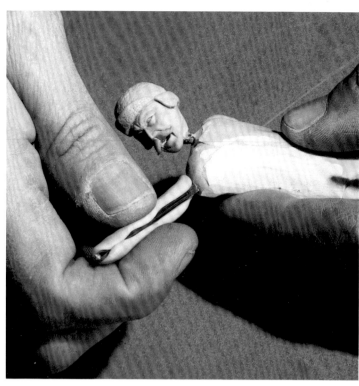

Take it to the lines then round the corners, making the body more oval than square.

Fill out the limbs by wrapping them with snakes of putty. You want to keep them thin for now, remembering that there will be a layer of clothing.

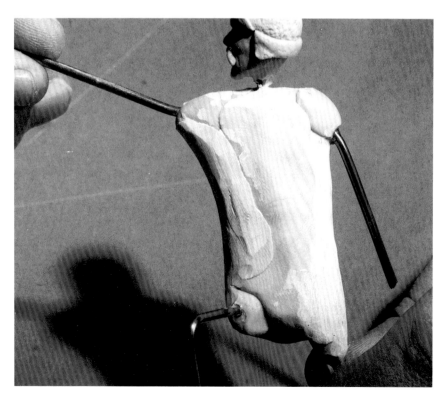

The result of the power shaping.

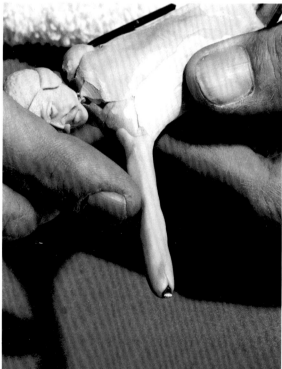

You don't need to worry about muscle contour at this point, but you do want to remember to put slight bends in the limbs, like here at the elbow, which were too small to worry about when setting the armature.

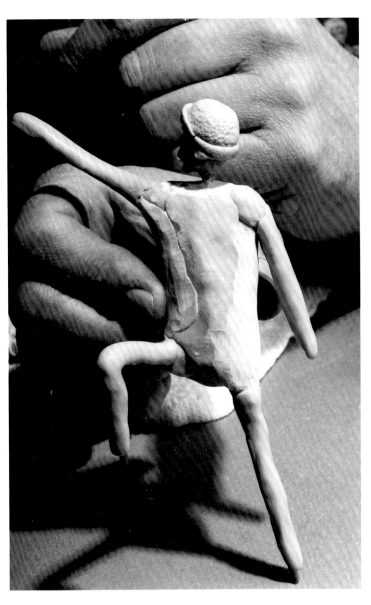

Take it to about this point and bake it.

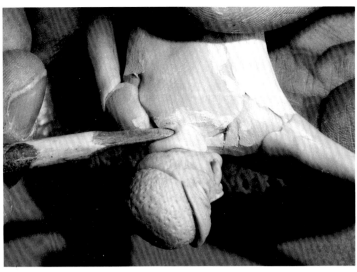

Work it in underneath. There will be excess to remove when it is in place.

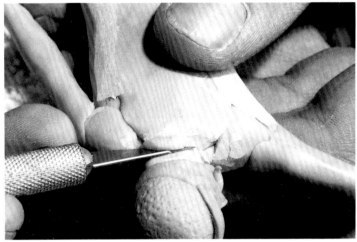

Thin it down by slicing off parts of it.

Work a roll of putty around the shoulders to form the neck.

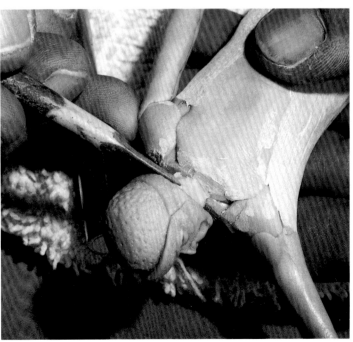

Smooth and sculpt it.

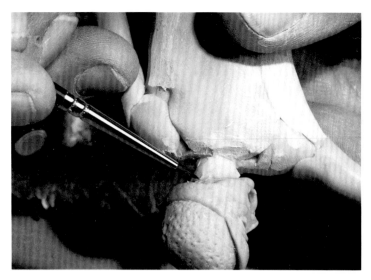

A brush will help you smooth where a tool will not reach.

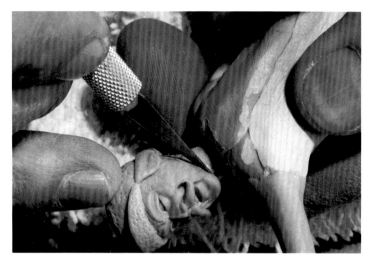

Clear an area for an Adam's apple, where the head will come down and meet it.

Add a little more beef to the back of the neck.

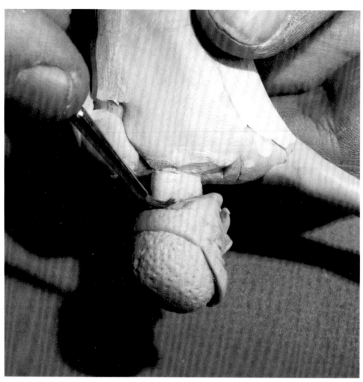

Smooth it off, blending the transition from the neck to the head.

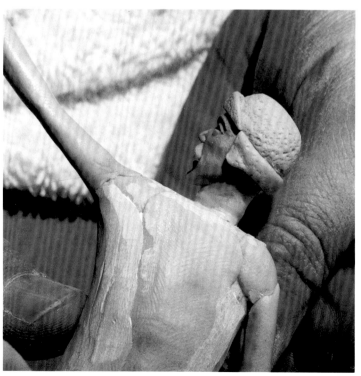

Ready for baking.

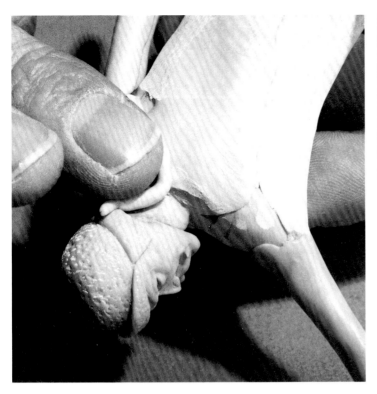

Apply a snake of putty to make the tendon of the neck. This goes from the collar bone to behind the ear. This will only show on the front side of the figure, the back being covered by clothing. I like to create figures that tell stories, and dramatic touches, like active postures and stretched tendons, add excitement to the story the figure tells.

Cut the snake to length and work it into place.

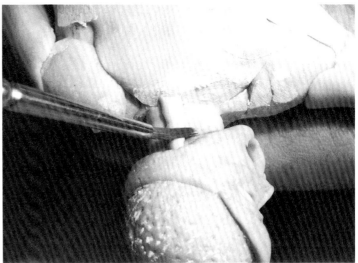

Use a paint brush to fair it in with the neck.

The finished tendon.

Refer to your sources for the uniform design. I sculpt my clothing in natural sections, dividing parts at the points where seams and other structural elements would occur in reality. I start with the breast of the jacket, using a rolling motion to spread the putty around the body.

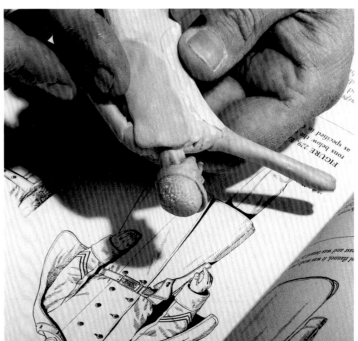

I cover more of an area than I ultimately want...

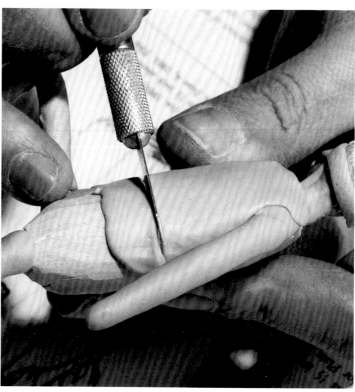

Trim the bottom at the belt line.

Folds run from points of tension. For example a bent elbow is the point of tension and the folds run away from it. The outstretched arm is the point of tension on this coat so the folds run away from it. Press the fold in with the side of the tool.

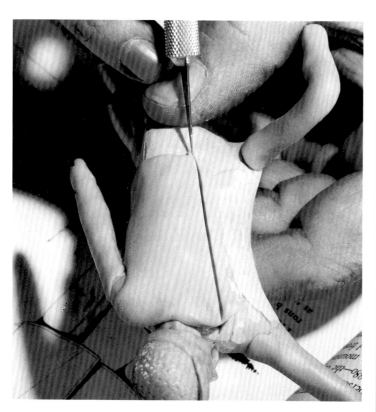

then trim it to size. The coat is double breasted and the opening comes in a slightly diagonal line across the body.

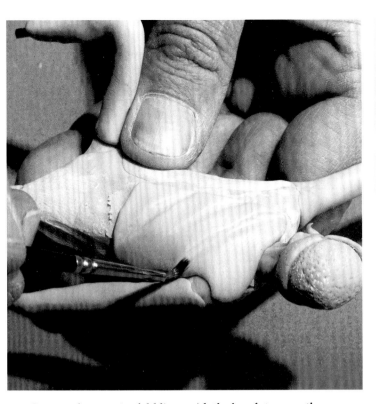

Go over these major fold lines with the brush to smooth them. Some of these will be covered by the cape.

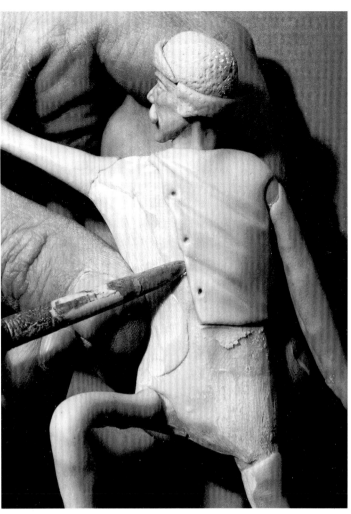

Between the buttons lift the edge of the coat.

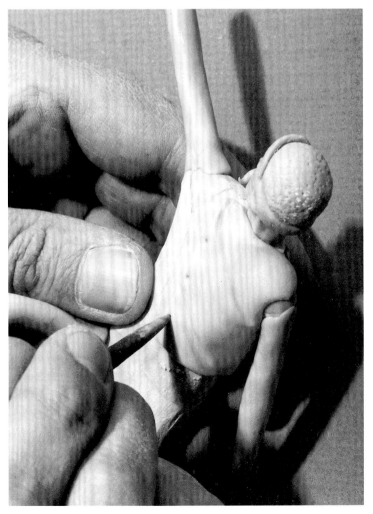

Define the location of the three buttons along the opening.

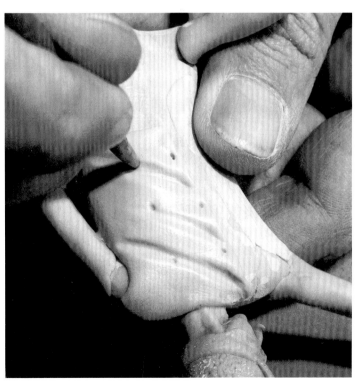

Define the position of the other three buttons.

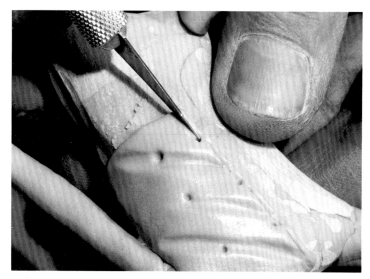

Scribe in the seams using a pressing motion with the blade. Dragging will deform the line. There is one seam just to the right of the coat opening. Make sure the edge is still lifted after you do the seam.

A second seam goes to the outside of the other row of buttons. You don't need to go to the shoulder because the cape will cover it.

Blouse out the bottom edge of the coat where the belt will lift it.

Ready to go back in the oven.

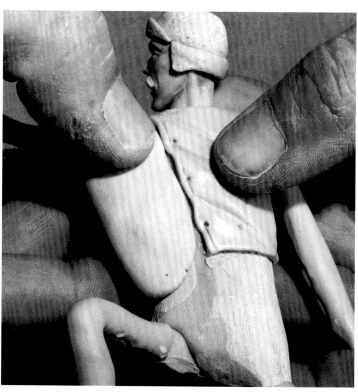

Work out the other side of the breast of the coat, keeping it thin near the opening. You will be working it up to and under the left side.

Trim it at the waist...

Smooth with a moistened finger.

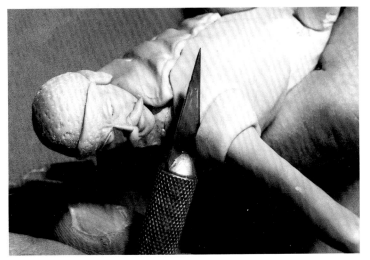

and at the seam of the sleeve.

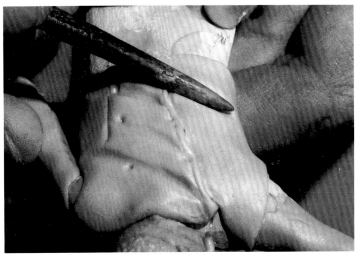

Create folds caused by the upraised arm, as you did on the other side of the coat.

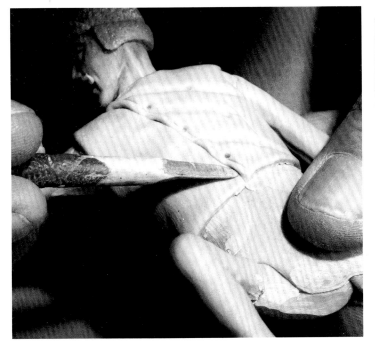

Work this edge underneath the left side.

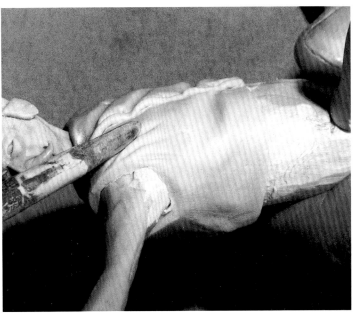

Smaller stress wrinkles come from the seam of the sleeve down the coat. Use the edge of the paddle tool for this.

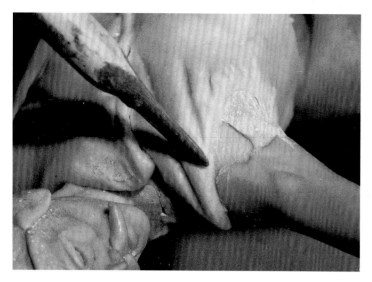

There are also small puckered folds where the material is gathered at the seam of the sleeve.

Impress the side seam and add some more puckered folds. along it.

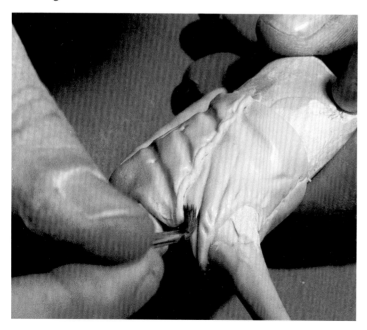

A moist brush will smooth the wrinkles while getting rid of the finger prints.

Blouse the coat out at the belt line.

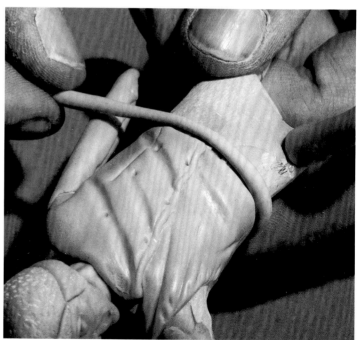

Lay on a snake for the belt...

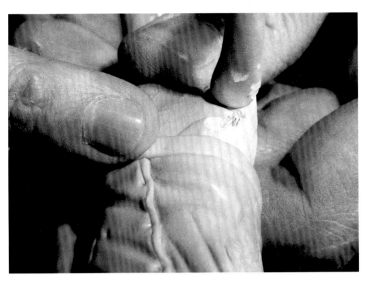

and flatten it into place.

With a blade make sure the top edge of the belt is flat.

A wider belt has the tendency to cup, so give this belt contour by pushing around the middle with side of the paddle.

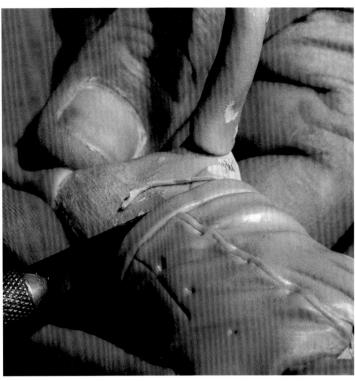

Cut off a nice crisp edge around the bottom.

Back in the oven.

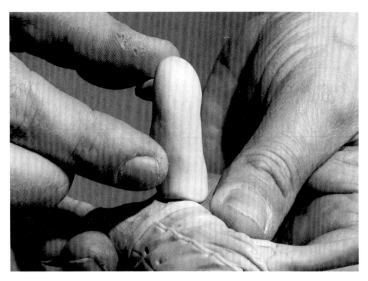

Add putty to the thighs and groin area for the pants.

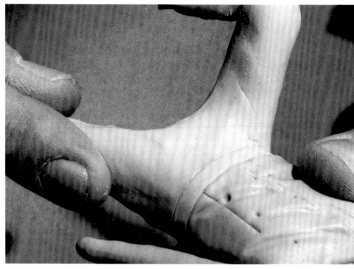

Smooth and shape further with a moistened finger.

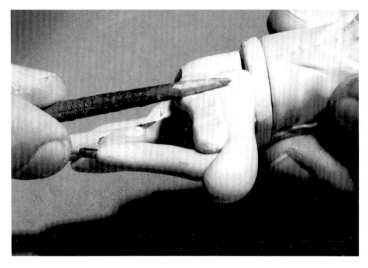

Work your way around the leg. Much of the back will be covered by a coat or by the base, so there is no need to waste putty or energy covering them.

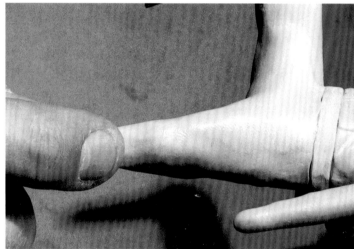

Give a hint of a knee joint on the left leg, thinning it down where it will go into the boot.

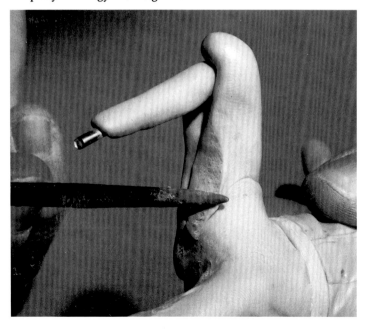

Blend and shape the pieces using a rolling motion.

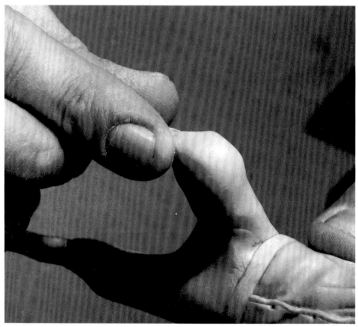

Do the same with the right leg.

Because the leg is lifted, there are tight wrinkles around the crotch. Use the edge of the paddle to press them in. It is important not to drag the wrinkles in. Dragging misshapes the putty and leaves a ridge on each side of the fold.

The right leg is a little long so we will establish this fold behind the knee before trimming it down.

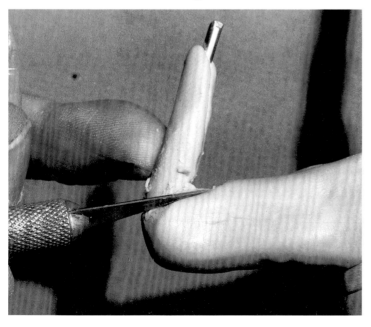

I'll cut the pant back on the lower leg now and file the leg when it has hardened.

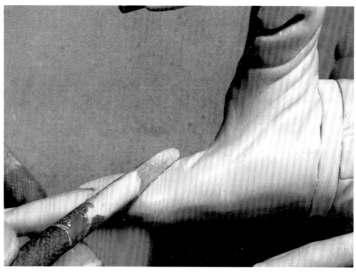

Continue with a few folds on the left leg.

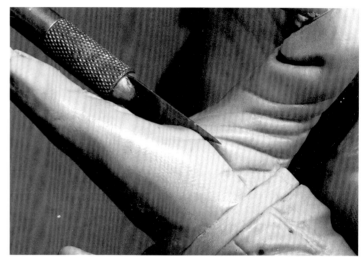

Cut in the fly of the pant...

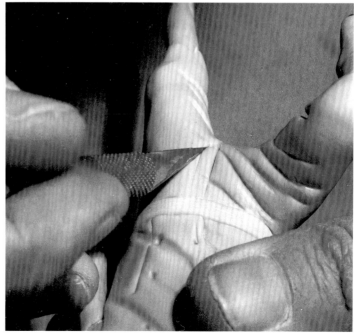

and its seam.

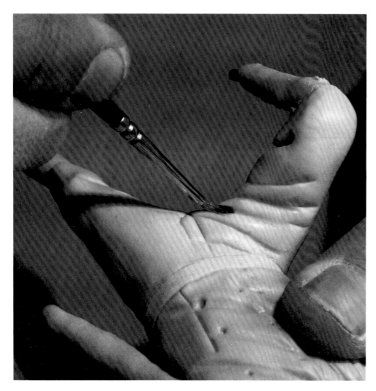

Smooth the wrinkles with the moistened brush.

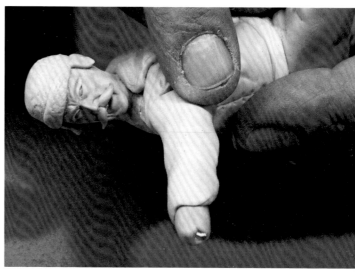

Work a roll of putty around the front of the right arm for a sleeve. Repeat on the back.

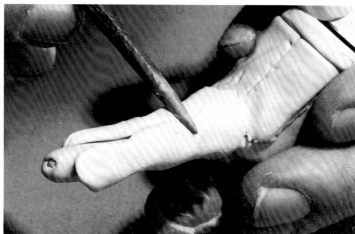

Roll the two pieces together. Remember this is a bulky overcoat. It is wool and has a quilt lining, so, while you don't want to make it too heavy looking, it must have some thickness.

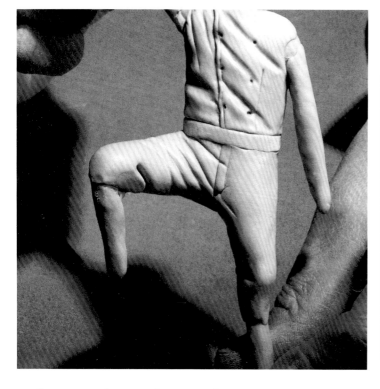

Progress on the pants. Pop it into the oven.

Add a piece at the armpit to show the pull of the fabric with the upraised arm.

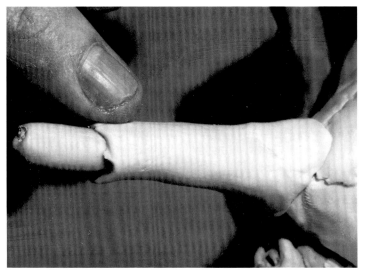

Smooth things out with a moistened finger.

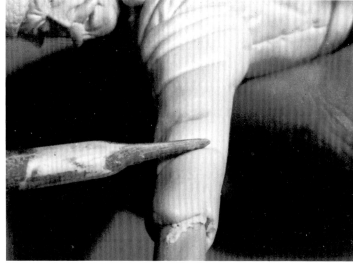

Continue adding wrinkles and folds.

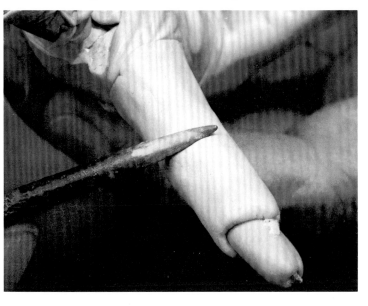

Establish the slight bend in the elbow. Though the arm is fairly straight, the elbow will be a source of tension on the clothing.

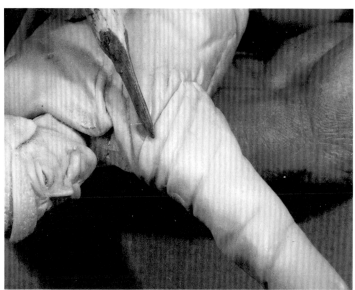

Come back and add a few pucker wrinkles along the seam.

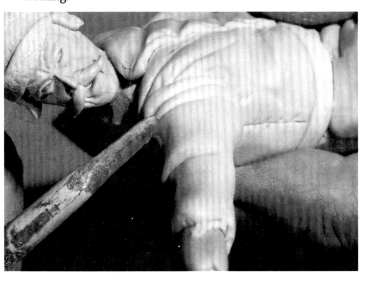

There are wrinkles at the shoulder where the raised arm would naturally bunch up the clothing.

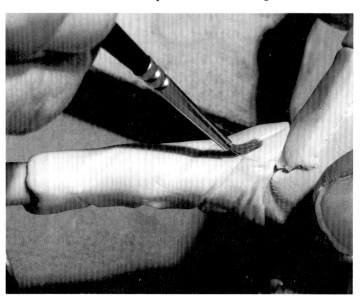

Smooth the wrinkles with a moist brush. This is a heavy material, so the wrinkles and folds will not be tight.

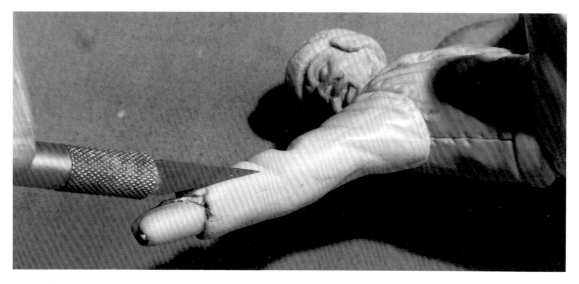

Add the seam lines, front...

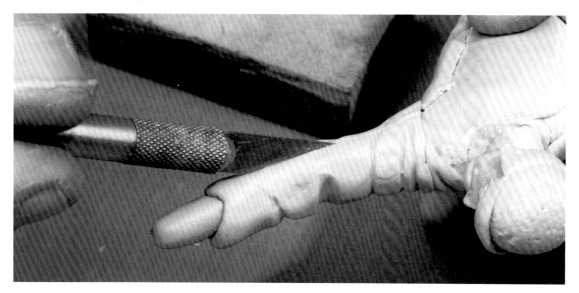

and back.

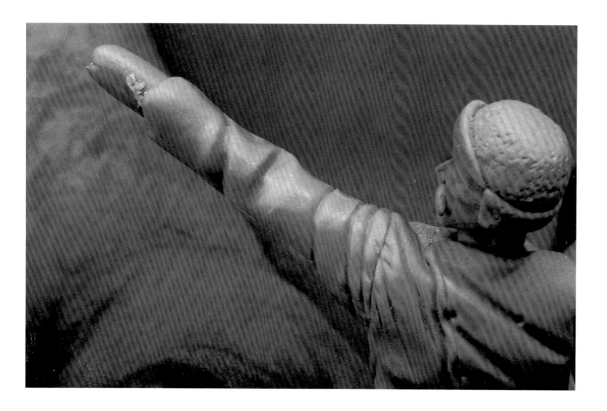

Ready for baking.

Smooth it with a moistened finger.

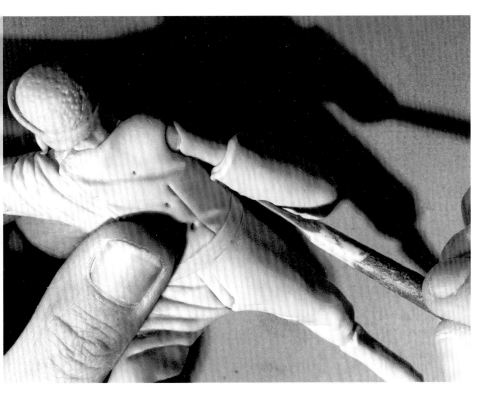

Work putty around the bottom portion of the left arm. The top portion will be hidden by the cape.

Not much of this sleeve will show, but you can add a few wrinkles. Put it in the oven.

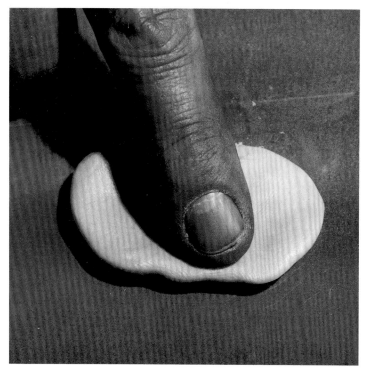

For the cape and coat tails you want the putty to be at the stage where it is almost set up, approximately 30-45 minutes after mixing. This will give it ability to be rolled into a thin sheet which can be laid over and folded back on itself to show the action of wind blowing the clothing. On a slick surface, work the putty out from the center to get a disc. It doesn't have to be too thin, though we will thin the edges when we put it on.

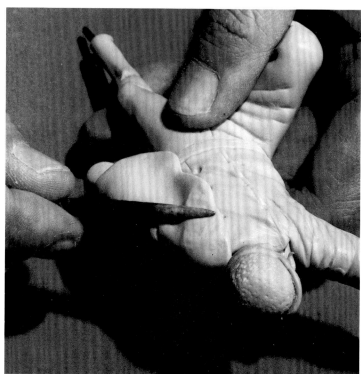

Drape it over the left shoulder.

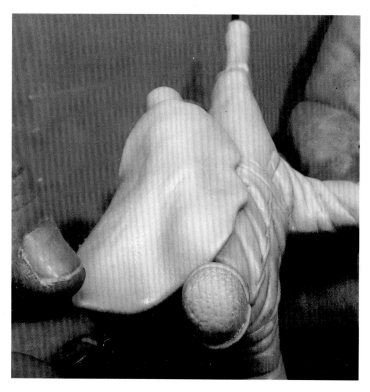

Roll the edge. Since the back will be hidden that is the direction we roll the excess.

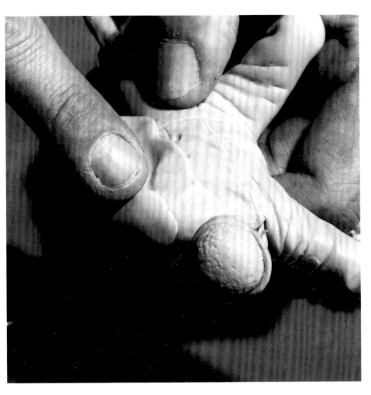

This area on the upper arm was too thin and about to tear through, so I add some putty back in, blending it with my finger.

The result.

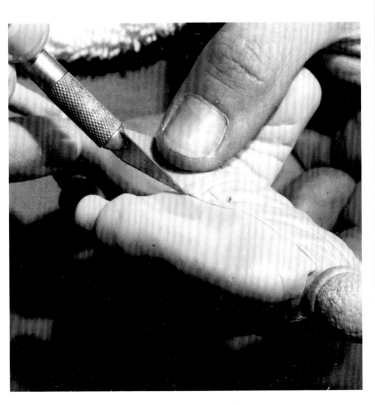

Cut the cape to shape, starting at the collar.

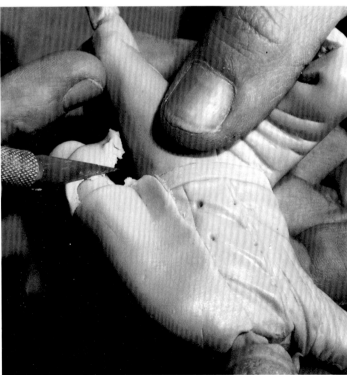

We want a square corner at the bottom of the cape and a line carried back over the arm. This corner will be flapping in the breeze.

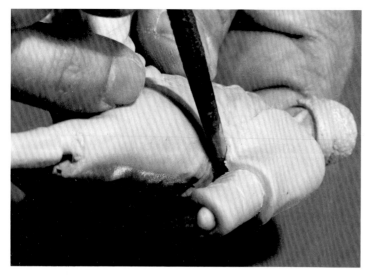

Reach under the cape at the corner and gently pull it away from the body. You may need to use a knife to relieve it.

Being careful not to push the cape back into the body, gently add some folds coming down from the collar.

When it is away from the body you can shape it with moistened fingers.

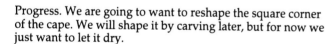

Progress. We are going to want to reshape the square corner of the cape. We will shape it by carving later, but for now we just want to let it dry.

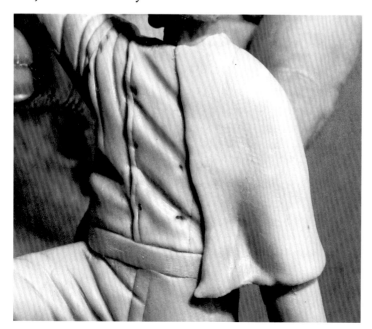

Smooth them out.

I've marked the places where the cape needs to be cut off and where the cuffs need to be thinned to accept the gauntlet.

Add button holes in the cape by pushing the knife in and rolling it over.

Progress. When you are working with a piece of clothing that comes away from the body like this, it is best to let it air dry, checking it often for sag. The oven tends to soften the epoxy and can create problems. Prop it in a position that will allow the fold to hang away from the body. When it has set up some you can push it into place and it will stay.

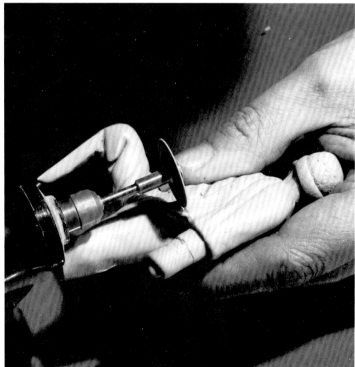

Cut the cape. If you make this cut at an angle, it will have a thinner look.

Change to a sanding drum to thin the cuffs of the sleeve.

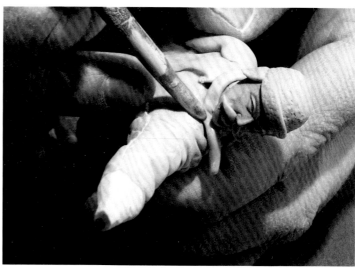

Press it into shape...

Thin the cuffs to a cone.

smooth it out...

Wrap a snake around the neck for the collar.

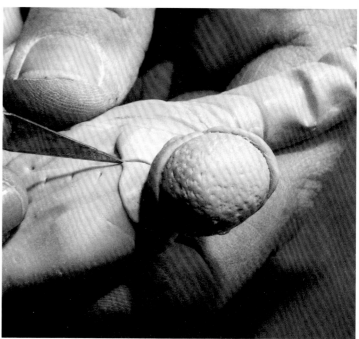

and cut it to size, opening at the front.

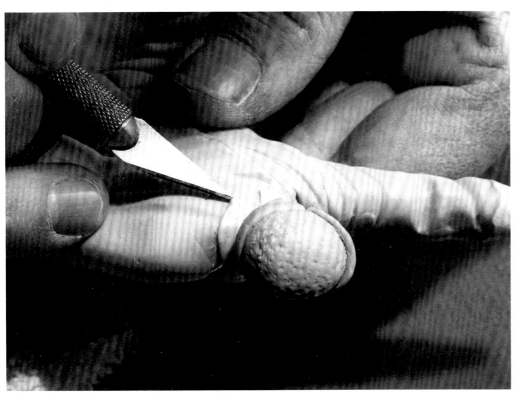

Undercut the corners and lift them up to give the collar a three dimensional look.

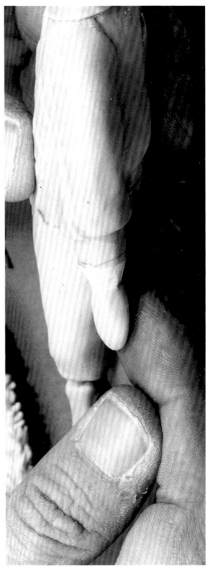

Before baking add a blob of putty that will become the left hand. Bake and cool the piece before continuing.

The result.

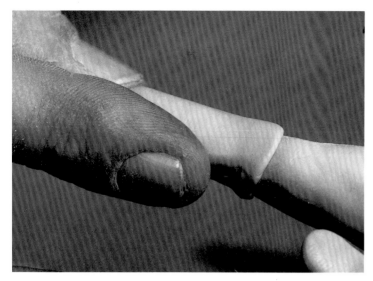

Work putty around the lower leg. The boots need to be thin to simulate boot leather and they have high tops. I'll work the putty as thin as possible, but I may have to come back and sand it down. The back will be hidden so we're not really concerned with it.

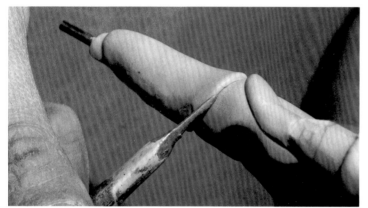

Shape the boot top.

Add folds to the boots. When made into a boot top, leather tends to collapse on itself.

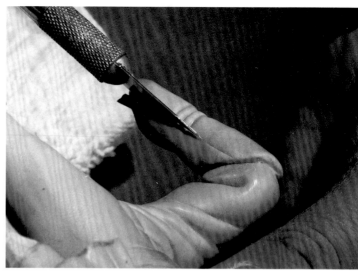

Add seams down the sides.

Ready for baking. The boots are a little long, but will be trimmed later.

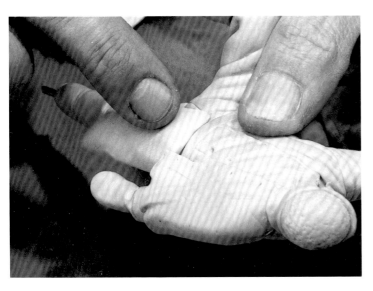

The left coat tail begins as a thick snake of putty. Work it up to the belt.

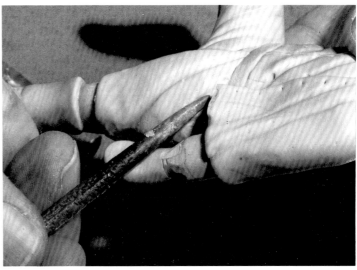

Add wrinkles coming down from the belt, following essentially the same line as the wrinkles across the chest.

Work it out with the finger.

Add some gathered puckers under the belt.

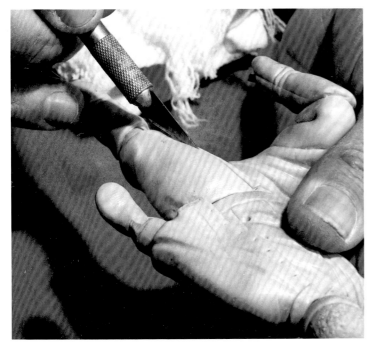

Trim it to fit.

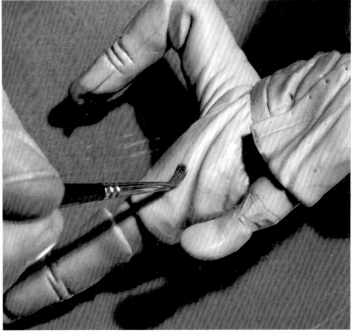

Smooth the folds with a brush.

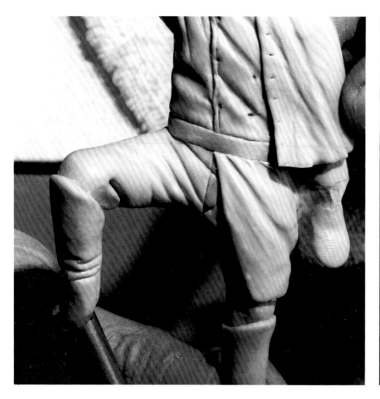

Progress.

Lift until it comes back on itself. Where the coat touched the leg be sure to scrape off the extra putty.

The last step before turning up the corner of the coat is to add the seam lines. They are continuations of the seams in the upper coat.

Undercut and lift the corner of the coat at the same time.

Brush the underside of the coat to make it smooth.

Add the seam for the lining where the coat is blown back.

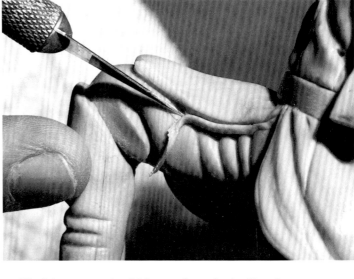

Work it out to a nice thickness, then trim it off to size.

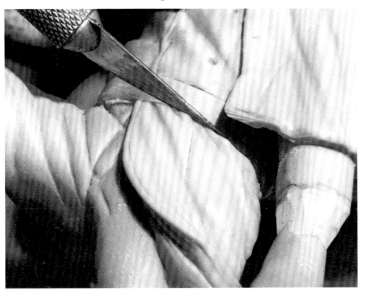

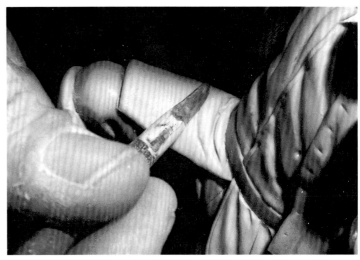

Add some folds where the leg is raised.

The bottom of the coat must come up to the belt. If you press down at the edge of the belt, you should get a good line.

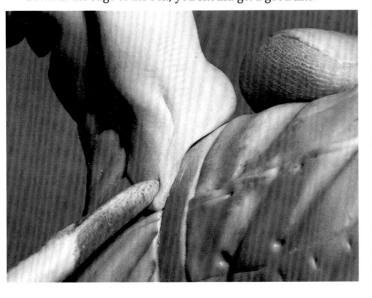

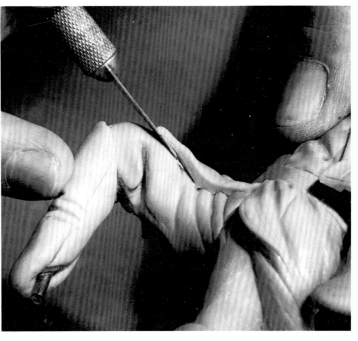

Do the other coat tail in the same way, making sure it meets the other side under the belt.

Undercut the coattail...

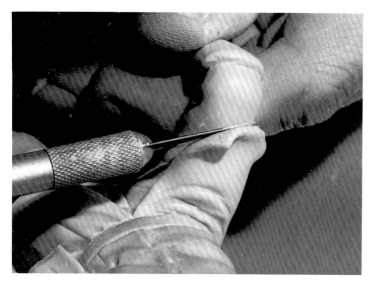

and turn it back on itself.

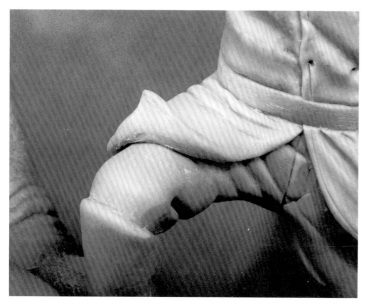

Ready for the oven.

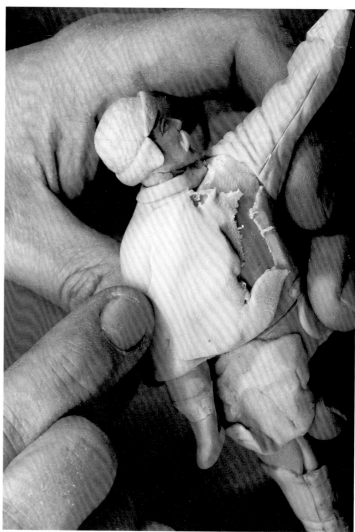

Blend it with the existing cape.

Since you can see the upper part of the back I need to fill it in. Work in this part of the cape.

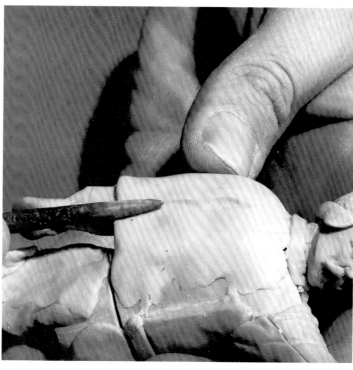

Add a deep fold where the arm would pinch the cape.

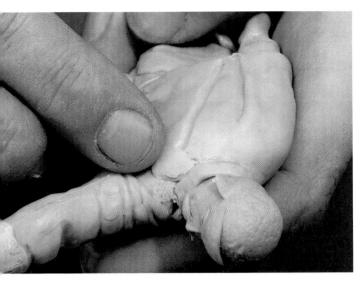

Add other wrinkles and make sure that the cape comes up under the collar.

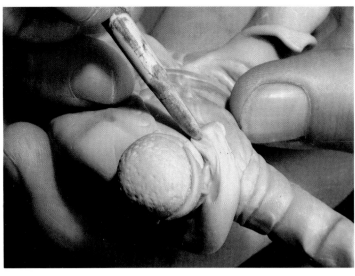

Work in a snake of putty for the turned back portion of the cape. Again, bring it up to the collar, so that it appears to go under the collar in the front, where it is attached.

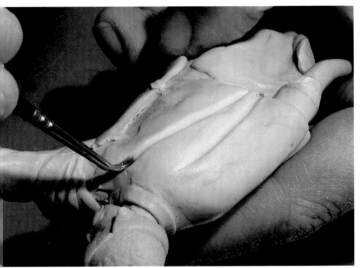

Smooth the wrinkles.

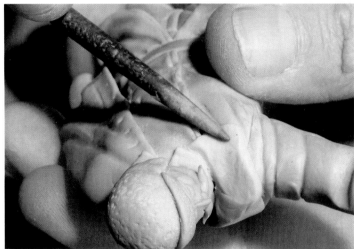

We also want to fold it back as if the wind has caught it. Begin by thinning it out...

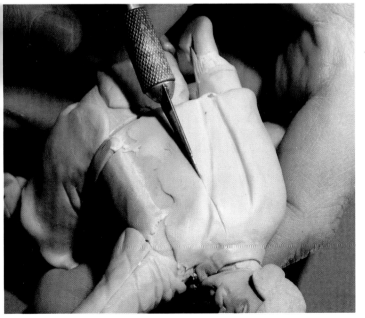

Add a seam down the middle, then bake it.

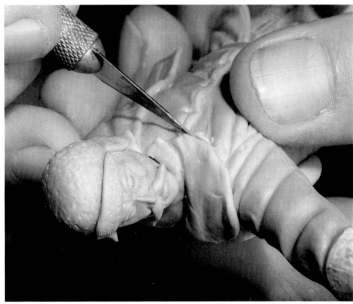

and trimming it to shape.

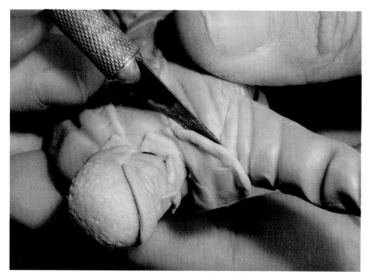

Lift the cape and turn it back.

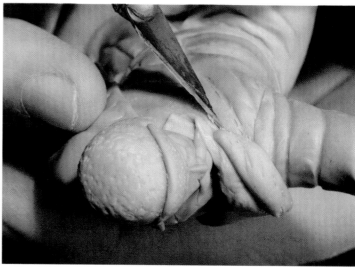

When I get the cape turning back the way I want it, I can add some extra cloth to the shoulder to beef it out. Work this in and blend it.

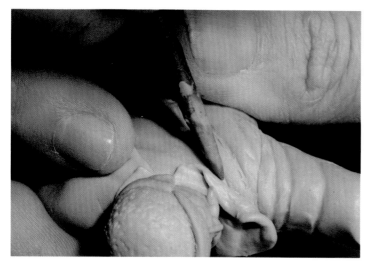

Work on the curl, so that it looks like it is coming from beneath the collar and the wind is blowing it back.

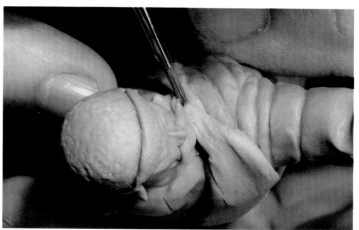

Smooth the joined area.

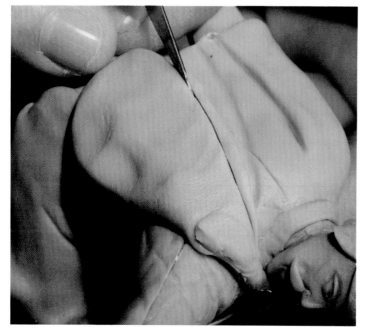

Trim the edge of the cape in the back.

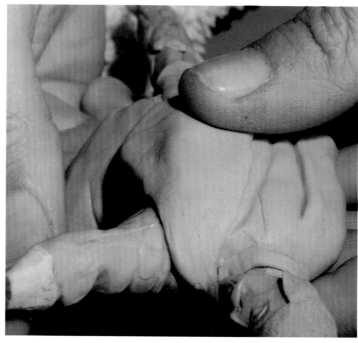

Thin the edge of the cape in the back...

and do a final trim.

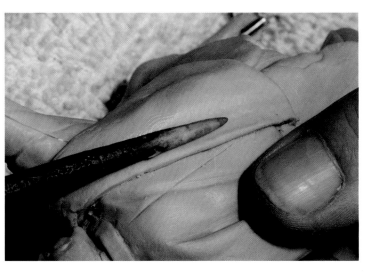

Make some folds in the cape. This one is wide, and is made by rolling the tool toward the edge.

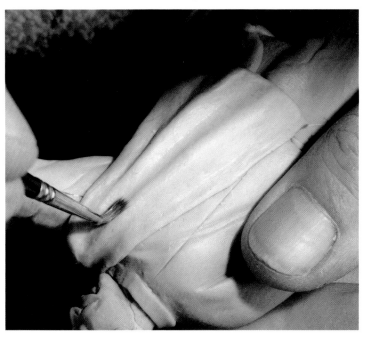

Add the other folds and smooth things out.

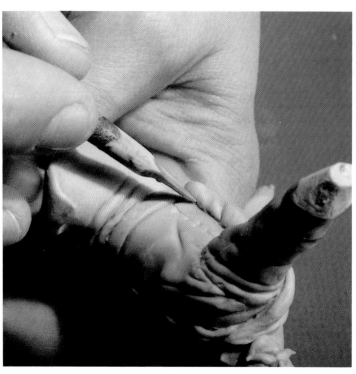

Add some wrinkles to the edge that can be seen from the front, undercut to give it some dimension. Bake it.

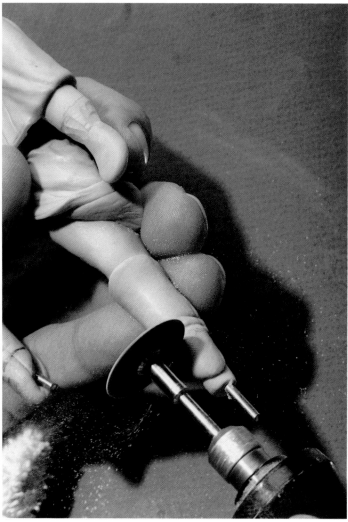

Cut off the left boot top at the bottom of the ankle.

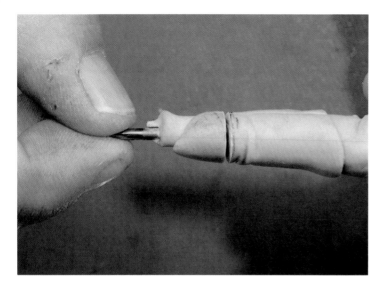

Cut through the putty down to the rod, leaving the rod intact. This technique is also helpful if you make a mistake and want to remove a part while leaving the armature.

Twist the excess off the armature.

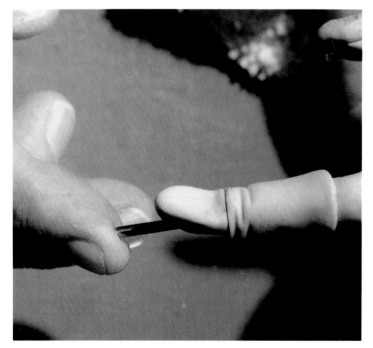

Add a bit of putty as the base of the foot.

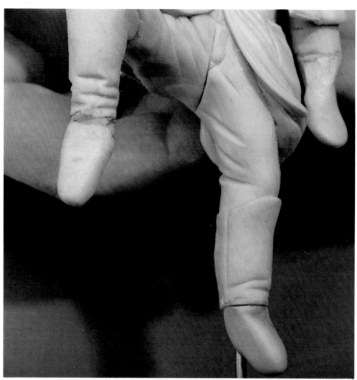

Apply putty to the other foot. Because of the angle of this figure's right foot, we can just add the putty to the end of the leg. If it were a more acute angle we would follow the same steps we did on the left foot.

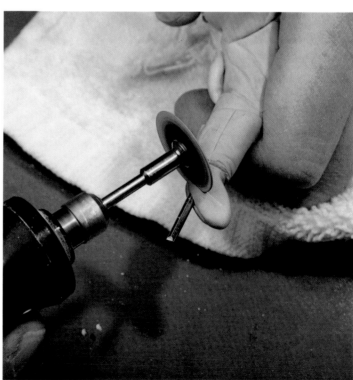

Shape the foot. Begin by cutting the foot flat, going through the wire as you do so. This is a particularly dangerous step, so be sure to wear safety glasses to protect your eyes from flying debris.

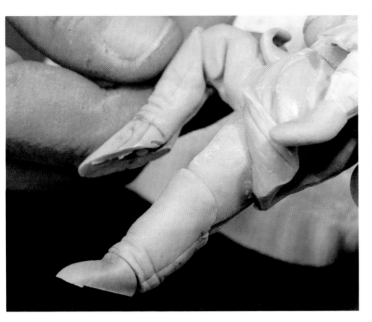

The feet cut. If it were a standing figure I would have left the wire to connect the figure to the base.

Establish the basic shape of the foot.

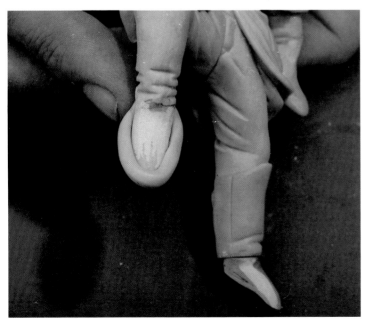

Add a bead of putty around the sole of the foot.

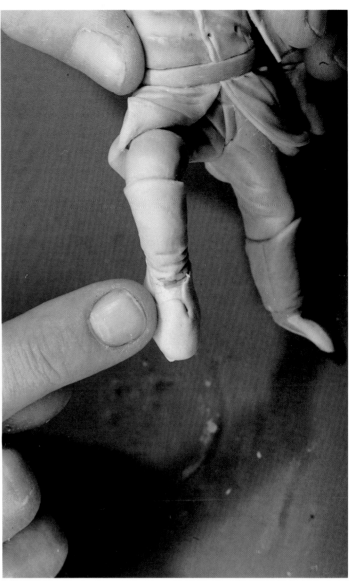

Work the putty from the bottom of the shoe to the top.

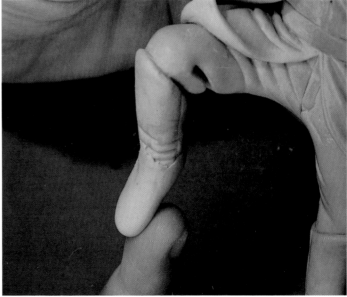

The excess you push under the foot to be ground off later. This helps keeps the foot nice and thin.

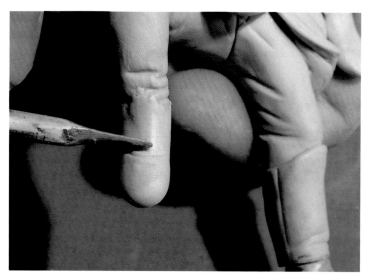

Add a couple of slight bends across the instep. Don't do too much or it begins to look unnatural.

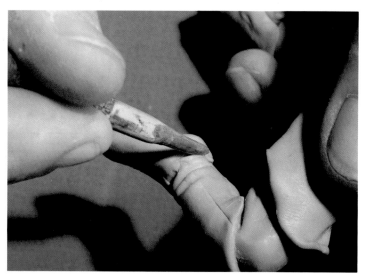

There will be bends above the heel where the foot is bent.

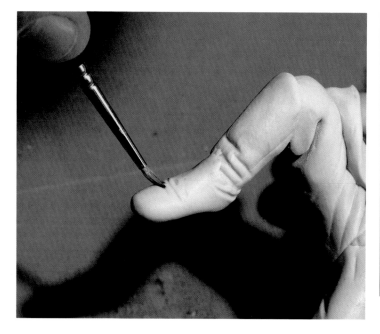

Brush out the folds.

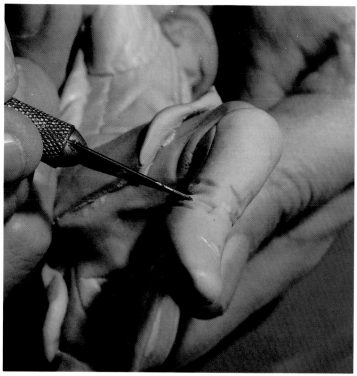

Cut along the line of the seam that divides the shoe portion of the boot and the upper portion.

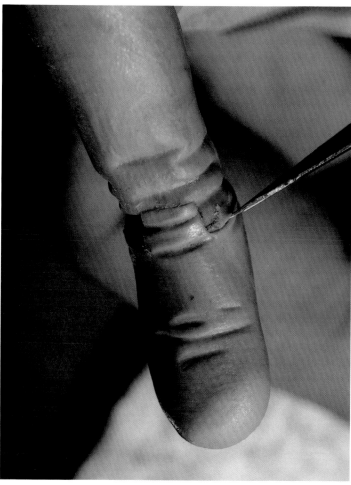

This boot had a rise over the instep, sort of like a tongue, that was sewn into the upper part of the boot and provided support at the bend.

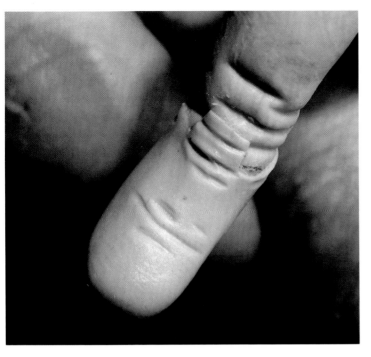

Ready for baking. This boot will have no sole because it is covered by the snow of the base. If it did it would be added to the shoe after baking this stage.

Create a base for building the hand by cutting between the fingers of the glove. This technique works when there is a gloved hand. If you were sculpting a bare hand you have to insert wire to build the fingers up.

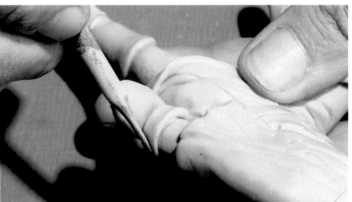

Add putty to form the cuff and hand parts of the glove.

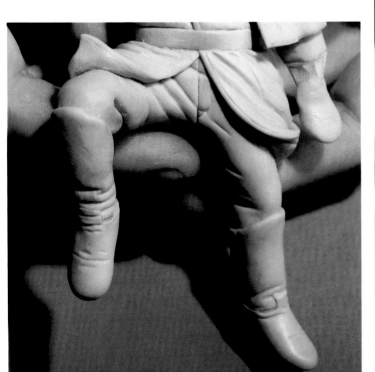

Completed boots.

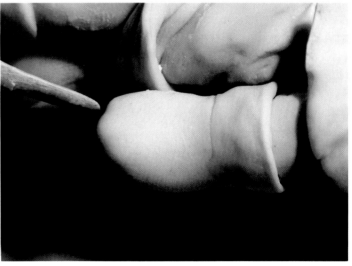

As you push the putty over the end of the hand, the finger marks begin to become clear.

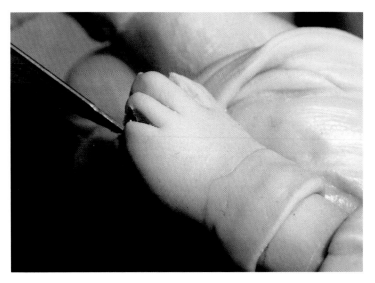

Remove the putty between the fingers.

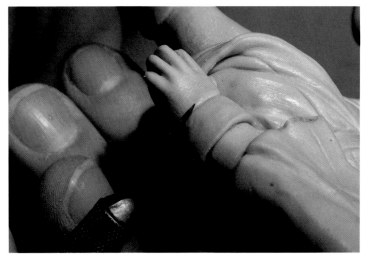

There is a seam where the gauntlet meets the glove.

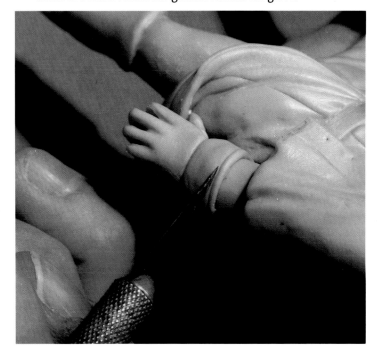

Another seam follows the edge of the gauntlet.

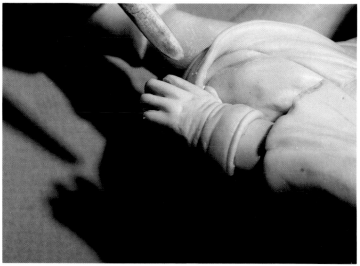

Add some wrinkles across the back of the hand and above the knuckles.

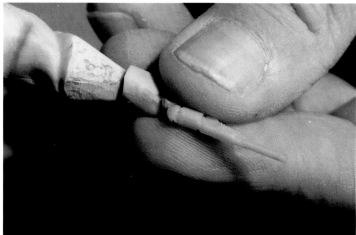

I use a commercial casting of a Colt pistol. To this is added a blob of putty, which I now glue to the right arm.

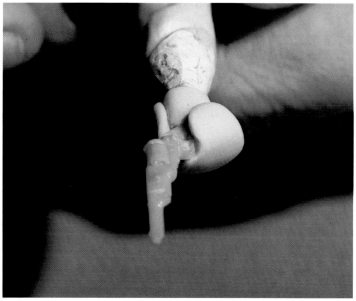

Work putty around the gun hand. In this formative stage you can work the hand like a mitten, particularly when it is grasping something.

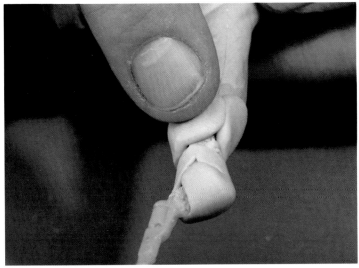

Add the cuff so it joins at the bottom of the wrist.

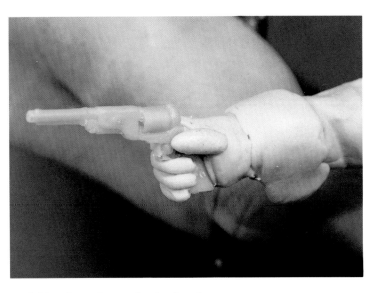

Add a piece of putty for the thumb...

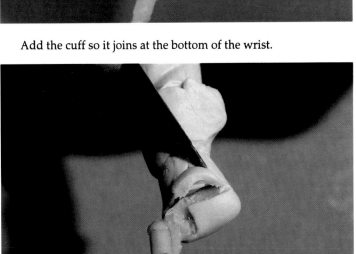

Trim the fingers to length.

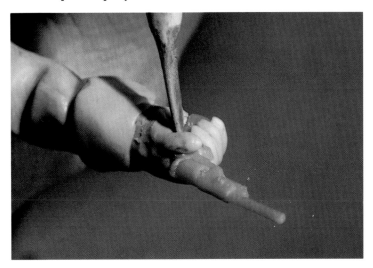

and work it into shape.

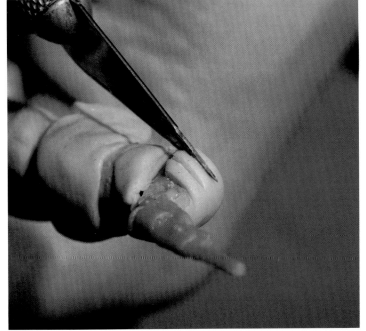

When the basic shape is established, separate the fingers.

Trim the gauntlet

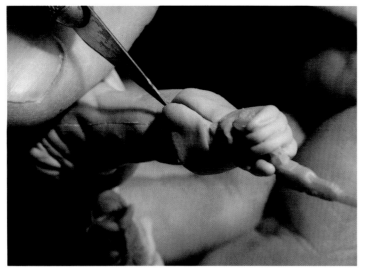

Split the gauntlet under the arm.

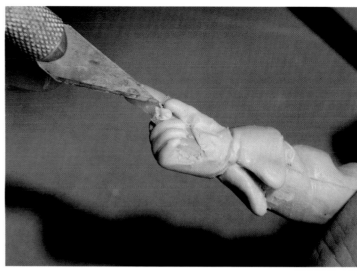

Add a trigger finger coming out of the trigger guard.

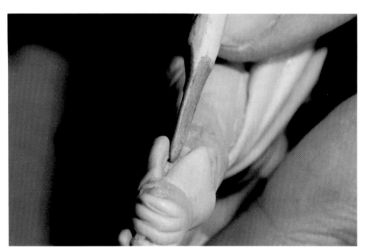

Open up the split.

Add wrinkles to the glove and smooth them with the brush.

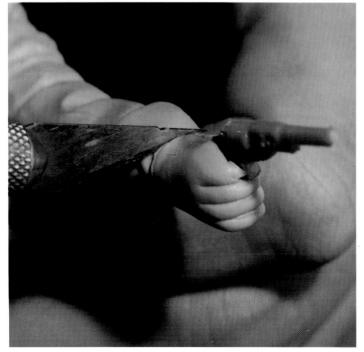

Create the seam between the glove and the gauntlet.

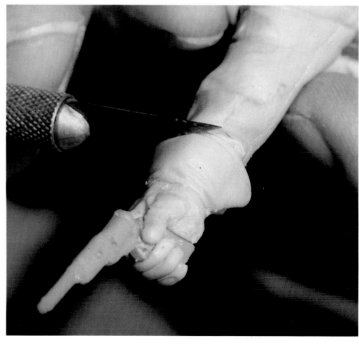

Put the seam line around the cuff.

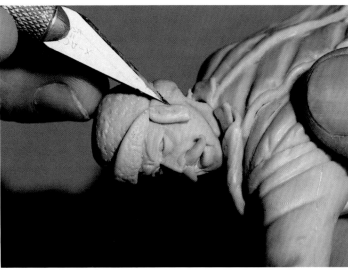

The details begin with the hair. It hangs from behind the hat and looks kind of scruffy. Work a roll of putty above the collar.

Do the sideburns in the same way.

Trim it down to overlap the collar just a touch.

Rather than try to define every hair, I pull out sections of hair for texturing. If you lift as you pull out, and remove some areas of hair, it gives you an uneven, natural, windblown look.

The results.

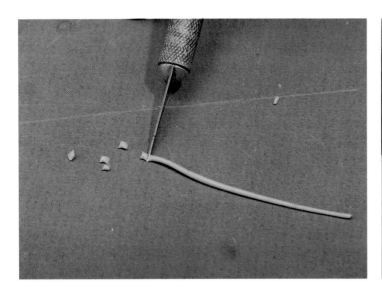

Cut buttons from a thin snake of putty.

and smash them out a little bit. Don't worry about getting them perfectly round at this point.

Roll them into balls...

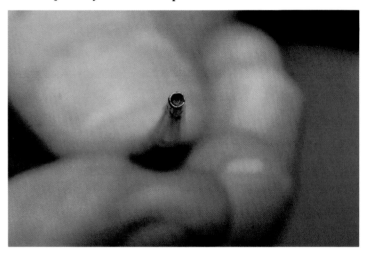

The buttons are shaped by the socket of a paint brush with the hair removed.

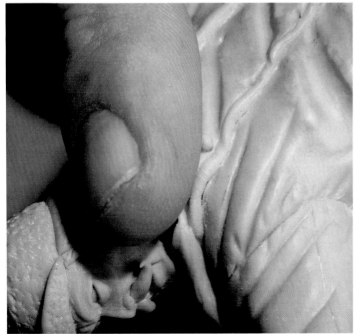

put them in place...

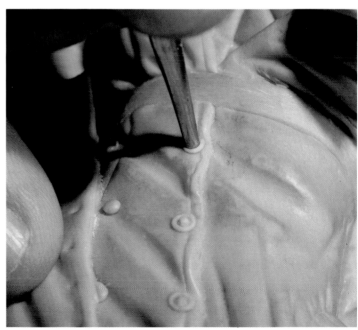

Press it in the center of each button...

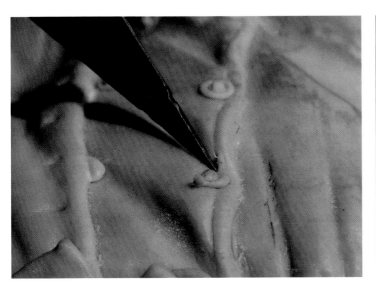

and come back with the knife and pull the excess away.

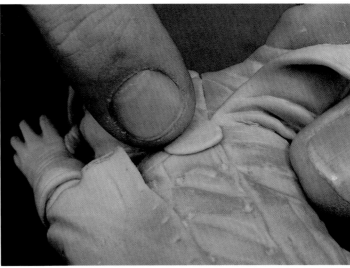

Apply a blob of putty to the belt buckle...

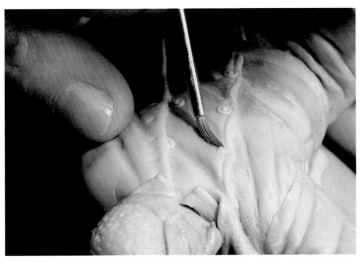

Clean it up with the brush.

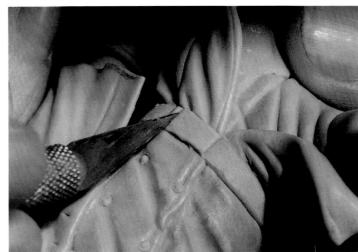

and trim it to shape.

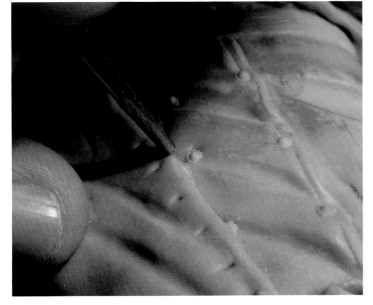

Go over the buttons again with a smaller brush socket. This gives them a small rim. This detail adds to the sculpture, but a lot of it can be done with paint, so only carry it as far as you think is reasonable.

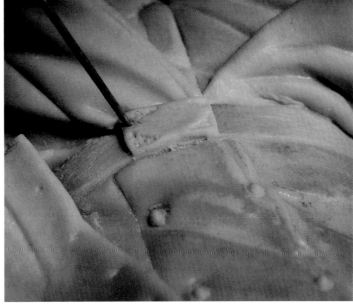

The buckle has an oval in the center. Bring this out by pricking around the edge with a pin.

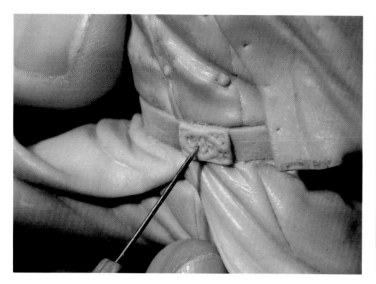

Use the same technique to create the U.S. in the center of the oval. Bake the figure for the last time.

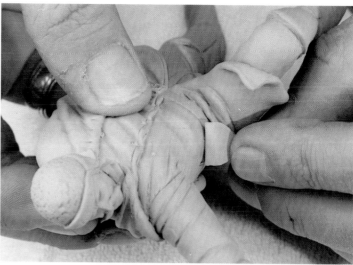

Form and apply a holster to the belt.

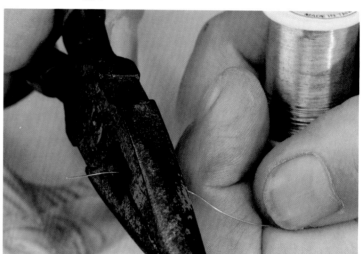

The strap for the cap is from spool wire. Cut a piece at the appropriate length.

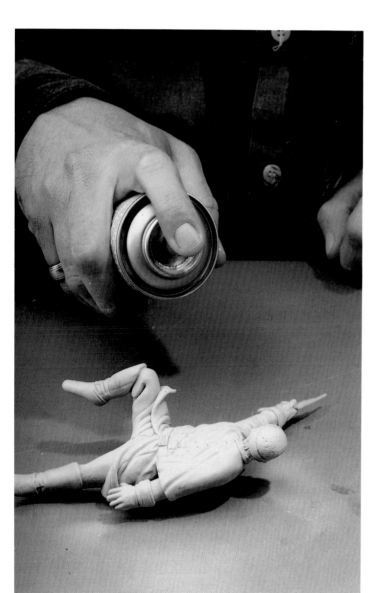

Prime with a spray paint.

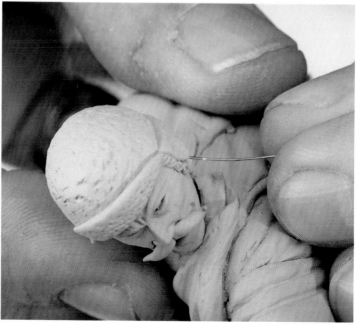

Shape to give it some action and glue to the flap.

THE FINISHED SCULPTURE

The stand is a small column that has been cut on a diagonal.

The snow is formed from light weight spackle, and accented
with grasses made from a short length of jute rope.

The arrow is formed from wire and is inserted into the leg.
The vanes are cut from metal.

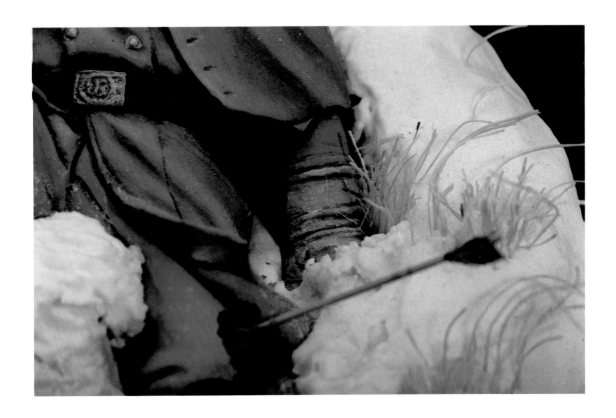

GALLERY OF KIM JONES'S SCULPTURES

"Fire on the Mountain." *From the collection of Steve Scott.*

"Operation Market Garden." *From the collection of Jeff Hudson.*

"Joe D. Maguire, 321st Air Transport Sqdn., Le Bourget,
France, Dec. 1944." *From the collection of Jon Maguire.*

"Captain, Luftwaffe, 1940." *From the collection of Tom Kirk.*

"Welcome Home, Debden, 1944." *From the collection of Jon Maguire.*

"Bad Luck on the Rosebud." *From the author's collection.*

"Dolph, 490th Bomb Sqdn., Burma Bridge Busters." *From the collection of Jon Maguire.*

"Sergeant, Royal Air Force, 1940." *From the collection of Tom Kirk.*

"High Summer Incident." *From the collection of Jon Maguire.*